GENEOLOGY

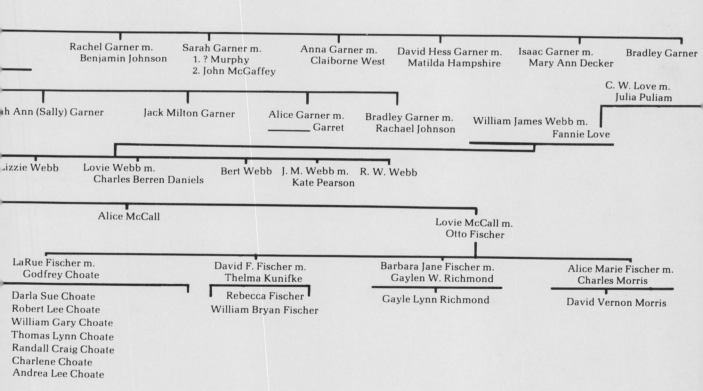

Rachel Garner m.
Benjamin Johnson

Sarah Garner m.
1. ? Murphy
2. John McGaffey

Anna Garner m.
Claiborne West

David Hess Garner m.
Matilda Hampshire

Isaac Garner m.
Mary Ann Decker

Bradley Garner

C. W. Love m.
Julia Puliam

h Ann (Sally) Garner

Jack Milton Garner

Alice Garner m.
——— Garret

Bradley Garner m.
Rachael Johnson

William James Webb m.
Fannie Love

Lizzie Webb

Lovie Webb m.
Charles Berren Daniels

Bert Webb

J. M. Webb m.
Kate Pearson

R. W. Webb

Alice McCall

Lovie McCall m.
Otto Fischer

LaRue Fischer m.
Godfrey Choate

David F. Fischer m.
Thelma Kunifke

Barbara Jane Fischer m.
Gaylen W. Richmond

Alice Marie Fischer m.
Charles Morris

Darla Sue Choate
Robert Lee Choate
William Gary Choate
Thomas Lynn Choate
Randall Craig Choate
Charlene Choate
Andrea Lee Choate

Rebecca Fischer
William Bryan Fischer

Gayle Lynn Richmond

David Vernon Morris

MR. MAC

THE MEMOIRS AND PHILOSOPHY OF A COUNTRY LAWYER

by LeRoy McCall

A humorous autobiography which contains something of interest to everyone. In a uniquely witty and readable fashion, this self-educated author, born in 1892, comments on Southeast Texas history, the law, philosophy, religion and today's society.

Library of Congress number
77-088847

Printed by Taylor Publishing Company
Dallas, Texas

CONTENTS

APPRECIATION   5

INTRODUCTION   6

1	FAMILY HISTORY	7
2	THE HOMESTEADERS	13
3	PROVIDENCE RICE	17
4	GEORGE WASHINGTON AND THE CHERRY TREE	20
5	WHEN THE ANTS GOT OUR DINNER	23
6	THE RICE INDUSTRY IMPROVES	26
7	RETURN TO THE OLD HOMESTEAD	30
8	GETTING OUR LIVING FROM THE SOIL	33
9	HURRICANES AND MOSQUITOES	40
10	THE HORSE AND THE PROPER WAY TO BREAK HIM	43
11	THE FIDDLE AND THE ODORIFEROUS ORGAN	49
12	FROM DISASTER TO WEALTH	53
13	THE DISCOVERY OF OIL IN BEAUMONT	57
14	THE ORANGE BOOM	60
15	THE FIG BOOM	62
16	THE FORTY-FIVE SO BIG IT SAVED MY LIFE	66
17	HUNTERS' PARADISE LOST	72
18	THE VILLAGE BLACKSMITH	85
19	A COUNTRY BOY IN NEW YORK	88
20	EDUCATION UNDER DIFFICULTIES	92
21	WHY DID I STUDY LAW?	99
22	HOW LAWYERS ARE MADE	103
23	CASE WON ON THE TEN COMMANDMENTS	105
24	CASE LOST	109

25	WHO STOLE THE BOLIVAR CATTLE?	113
26	LEADING QUESTIONS PAID OFF	116
27	TO WHOM DID THE COW BELONG?	120
28	OUR LIBERAL HOMESTEAD LAWS	123
29	LIBERAL DIVORCE LAWS OR TRIAL MARRIAGES	126
30	MAMA, CAN I SAY "HELL" TO THAT MAN?	132
31	THE LAND TITLE THAT CHECKED BACK TO GOD	134
32	A CASE WON BY THE DICTIONARY	136
33	CROSS-EXAMINATION — THE SMOKING PISTOL	138
34	RACE RELATIONSHIPS	140
35	IT IS NOT THE HIGH COST OF LIVING, BUT THE COST OF HIGH LIVING	143
36	TRIBUTE TO WOMANHOOD	146
37	RELIGION AND PHILOSOPHY	148
38	OPTIMISTIC VIEWPOINT	153
39	CONCLUSION AND ADVICE TO THE YOUNG LAWYER	154
40	INDEX	158

APPRECIATION

I cannot publish this book without expressing my appreciation for the contributions which made it possible. First, I appreciate the fact that Providence has granted me a long life and preserved my memory to the extent that I can record happenings of the past eighty years.

I express my appreciation to my several secretaries who participated in the typing, and especially to Shirley Vaughn of my Anahuac office who urged me to write this book.

This work would have been impossible without the faithful assistance of my sister, Alice McCall, who is a retired school teacher of forty-seven years of teaching experience and who, although eighty-three years of age, has the clear mind of a much younger person.

Also, I must express appreciation to my wife, Mary Sandell McCall, to whom I was married for forty-nine years and who contributed much to this work before her death in August 1975.

To my host of friends and clients who have contributed to a full and interesting life I express my deep appreciation.

LeRoy McCall

INTRODUCTION

Now that it is January 1, 1976, and I will be eighty-four years old next month, and still having a fair memory of things that transpired in the preceding three-quarters of a century, I have resolved to set down some of the happenings of the era in this area. I ask the reader to pardon the frequent use of the personal pronoun, as this will necessarily be more or less the history of my own life, with many sidelights that affect others. Perhaps an old person is inclined to want to talk too much, resulting in a wounded vanity if no one listens. By writing, this stigma is removed because if you get tired of this and throw it in the wastebasket, I will not know it. My wife often told me that I talked too much, but my answer to this was, "I make our living talking and you have not been hungry for a long, long time." I am not writing this with a view of making money out of it. Fortunately, I do not need the money, and furthermore, I do not think it would have any monetary value. I am merely recording the events for what benefit it may be to the present or future generations. A record of what life was like 75 years ago may cause this generation to be more appreciative of what they have. I have been impressed by a remark of an old colored friend who has lived through the years that I have lived, under similar circumstances, whose philosophy I appreciate. He said to me some time ago, "I hear talk about the good old times, but if you want to know what I think, we have the good old times right now."

I am inclined to believe that modern luxuries have crept upon us so slowly that we take them for granted and fail to appreciate what modern science and human ingenuity have accomplished in the last three-quarters of the century for the benefit of mankind.

I have been thinking of making a record of these events for some time, but it is only recently that I have found the time for such trivial matters and that is because my son and able law partner, LeRoy McCall, Jr., has relieved me of many of the burdens of a busy country law practice.

CHAPTER ONE

FAMILY HISTORY

If this is to be a history of my life, I presume it should begin with my birth, which occurred, according to the record of the United States Census Bureau, which I have in my safe, on the 27th day of February, 1892, at Sabine Pass, Texas. Sabine Pass, as you may know, is a sleepy little town in almost the extreme southeastern portion of Jefferson County, the extreme southeastern county of the State of Texas. The town was named for Sabine Pass, which is a neck of water extending from Sabine Lake to the Gulf of Mexico. Sabine Pass is an old town. I have been told that prior to the Civil War there were numerous houses there, that ocean-going vessels landed and discharged their cargo for distribution by smaller vessels to the villages along the Sabine and Neches Rivers. As you know, it is the site of the old fort where Dick Dowling and his company of Irishmen acquitted themselves fairly well during the Civil War.

As to my ancestors, taking the paternal first, my father, Dave McCall (no better man ever lived and more will be said of him in a later chapter) was born at Sabine Pass on March 4, 1862. He was one of the five children born to John McCall and Martha McCall, who was born Martha Garner. We know little of the background of John McCall, my paternal grandfather. He must have come to Sabine Pass in the late 1850's or about 1860. He had a brother by the name of Jim McCall who came with him and I understand that their mother, who had remarried and then was named Frederickburg, came with them. I know nothing of the background of John McCall except that he died at his own hands about the year I was born. I often thought it was significant that my father, with whom I worked side by side for 20 years, never mentioned his father's name to me, respectfully, disrespectfully or otherwise. I do not want to seem disrespectful of my ancestors. If I inherited any good qualities from them, I appreciate it, but because of what has just been said above and what may be said later in this work, I have my suspicions as to why John McCall came to Sabine Pass.

As to my paternal grandmother, Martha Garner McCall, I know more about her because I remember her very well. I was in my early teens when she died and some of my most cherished early childhood memories are of the visits in her home. She was one of the seven children of Jacob Garner, who was born on the east side of Cow Bayou in what is now Orange County, across from the present town of Orangefield. Jacob Garner was one of the six children of Bradley Garner, who settled there, according to the deed records, in 1825. We have no record of where Bradley Garner originally lived.

As far as we know, three of his children went west in the early days and the other three went to Sabine Pass under circumstances as follows. One of the very early settlers of Sabine Pass was John McGaffey, who acquired a substantial amount of land and owned a large herd of cattle. Another of the early settlers was Ben Johnson. McGaffey must have been an Irishman; I understand that Johnson was a Dane. They were very hardy and probably seafaring people. I do not know that to be a fact, but a good many of the early settlers of Sabine Pass arrived there because it was a port.

As is well known to most students of Texas history, South Texas had thousands of longhorn cattle for which there was no market until the railroads crossed the continent and trail drives were begun to Kansas, with the exception of the limited market at New Orleans where ships would take them to the eastern seaboard. I have been told by old ranchmen that very often they would make a drive of cattle to New Orleans and there would be no buyers and no ships. The cattle would be killed for the hides and tallow and the carcasses thrown into the Mississippi River. At any rate, John McGaffey had large herds of cattle in the Sabine Pass country and had married Sarah Garner, a daughter of Bradley Garner. Sarah was an older sister of Jacob Garner, the father of my grandmother. Rachel Garner, another sister, had married Ben Johnson of Sabine Pass.

As my grandmother told it to me, when she was a child six years of age, which must have been sometime in the 1840's, John McGaffey, the husband of her Aunt Sarah, drove a herd of cattle to New Orleans and never returned. In that period of history that would be a hazardous trip especially if a cattleman was returning with money. The reason for his failure to return was never known. The widow, if she was a widow, sent for her younger

8

brother, Jacob Garner, the father of my grandmother, to come to Sabine Pass to take care of her cattle.

As I believe I stated above, he lived near Cow Bayou. As my grandmother told it, he cut logs, built a large raft and loaded all of his belongings, including chickens and children, on the raft, and poled down Cow Bayou into Sabine Lake and on to Sabine Pass. This was more than one day's journey and the only place to make camp was with an old Dutchman by the name of Pavel who lived on the banks of the Sabine Lake and was in the business of making split cypress shingles. They spent the night there. During their stay, many of the chickens had gotten away and there was trouble catching them. Finally, by mid-morning, everything, so they thought, was loaded and ready to go and they started poling the raft out into the lake. They were about 200 yards from shore, but my grandmother, who was then six years of age and who had been looking for shells up and down the lakeshore behind the bushes, was not aboard. As there were several children, she was not missed. When she came out from behind the bushes and old man Pavel saw that Mr. Garner had failed to load one of his children, he began to holler and wave his hands and said to Garner, "You have left one of your chillins." My grandmother's father thought he said "chickens" so he waved back and said, "Oh, I'll give that one to you, Mr. Pavel." My grandmother said that when she heard that, she did not fail to let her presence be known.

Jacob Garner lived his lifetime out at Sabine Pass. He died before I was born, but I well remember my great grandmother, old Grandma Garner, living in an old, old house with her one unmarried daughter, Sally. The place was right across from where the Sun Company tank farm is now, about a mile west of Sabine Pass. His children were as follows: Jack Garner, who was a carpenter and railroad man and lived in Beaumont (we visited his home many times); Molly Garner, who married Brad Johnson who was the son of the old Ben Johnson. They must have been first cousins. I remember Brad Johnson. He had a nice home, which was the last home on the old ridge going west from Sabine Pass. He did well, and left his wife a good home and about 300 head of cattle when he died of heart failure while in the marsh hunting ducks. Ducks were hunted for market in those days. I remember very well my father hunting ducks, going out early in the morning and coming back in the mid-morning with a horse loaded down with ducks. He had a ready market for them since Jules Boudreaux, the railroad station agent, purchased them at two-bits a pair, twelve and a half cents each, refrigerated them, and shipped them north. That seems like a very cheap price, but if a man could kill a hundred in a day, which they often did, that was about $10.00 above the cost of ammunition, and $10.00 was a lot of money in those

9

days. As said above, Brad Johnson died of heart failure while hunting ducks in the marsh for market. I've heard him say that it was hard work and he would not hunt ducks if he could not make $10.00 a day.

Another daughter of Jacob Garner was Alice. I believe that she was the youngest one and she married a Garrett. She lived out the latter years of her life at Fannett, Texas. Another child was Annie Garner, who married Jim McCall, the brother of my grandfather, John McCall. They had a nice home on the ridge and lived their entire lives at Sabine Pass. Another daughter was Sally, whom I understand never married. As I stated above, she lived at the old Garner place that her parents left. I will not, at this time, carry the paternal family tree any further.

As to my maternal grandparents, my mother, who was Sue Webb, was born either in the southwestern part of Tennessee or the northwestern part of Mississippi. At any rate, her father had a plantation in the Mississippi Delta in northwestern Mississippi. I've often heard her say that she was raised five miles from Memphis. Her father, W. J. Webb, was a member of the old antebellum aristocracy. He had a large plantation before the Civil War and, like many others of that era and generation, he was well educated, not in any profession, but only to be a Southern gentleman. He had a lot of Negroes and mules and worked for the United States government in the building of the Mississippi levee, for which he said he was never paid, as the war broke out before he got his money. As I recall, he served, not as an actual soldier, but in the commissary department in the Civil War. His wife was Fannie Love. There were six children and the oldest, I believe, was Lizzie, who died young, unmarried. The next was my mother. The next was Lovie Webb, who married C. B. Daniels, a civil engineer of Beaumont, after the family moved to Hamshire. The next was Bert Webb, who never married and died here in Hamshire some years ago. The next were twins, J. M. Webb and R. W. Webb. R. W. Webb never married and died many years ago, and J. M. Webb married and had a large family. His children and grandchildren now live in this area.

Conditions after the Civil War made a delta plantation unprofitable. My grandfather sold his plantation and came to Texas and bought a ranch. He returned home and told his family to prepare to move to Texas. His old mother was living with him at that time and she became terribly distressed and said, "Oh, Billy, it would kill me to move to that wild country." That so discouraged the old man that he came back to Texas and sold his ranch. The city of Forth Worth is on it now! He then went to Arkansas and bought thousands of acres of hardwood timber land and started a sawmill and, as he knew nothing about the sawmill business, went broke. In 1886 he moved to

10

Sabine Pass with his family, composed of two daughters, of which my mother was the oldest, and three teen-aged boys. He rented a house and set up housekeeping. Their home was about half a mile from the home of my father, Dave McCall, who was then a young man.

Soon after they arrived, the hurricane of 1886 struck Sabine Pass. My grandfather's family knew nothing about hurricanes and they did not leave their home and seek higher ground, as the oldtimers did. The water came up in the house and they all climbed into and spent the night in a mulberry tree, and saw the house wash away.

Of couse, this was a traumatic experience for people from Mississippi. I was told by my Aunt Lovie, my mother's youngest sister, that one of the most welcome sights she ever beheld in her life was that of old Hiram Stewart, a neighbor, who came wading through the waist-deep salt water, looking up into the tree. In other circumstances, the face of Hiram Stewart would not be a pleasant sight. I remember him very well from my childhood days and I thought he was one of the ugliest men I knew. Aunt Lovie said that at the time she thought him to be the handsomest man she had ever seen.

The storm of 1886 was very tragic as far as my father was concerned. My father's family, that is the children of John McCall and Martha McCall, was as follows: Dave McCall, my father, was the oldest and the next was Annie. Her tragic death will be related below. The next was Maggie, who became an old maid and in her later life married Jim Tyree. They both lived their lives at Sabine Pass. The next was Eva, who married Charlie McGaffey, the grandson of the old John McGaffey mentioned above, and they lived their lives at Sabine Pass. The youngest was Drew McCall, who worked for many years in the office of the Santa Fe Railroad at Galveston and finally moved to Houston and worked for the Gulf Oil Company until his death several years ago.

The 1886 storm took as many lives, in proportion to the population, as the 1900 storm in Galveston. Among the casualties was my Aunt Annie mentioned above, who had married Arthur McReynolds. As I have heard the story, they lived a short distance from where my father lived with his parents, and when the storm came and the water rose and got very high, Arthur tried to make his way with his wife, who was then pregnant, to her mother's home, which was considered a safer place. He did not succeed in reaching there with her, as she was washed out of his arms and lost. He survived. After the storm there was, of course, a search for dead bodies and it was told to me that my father found his sister on a little ridge in a marsh, miles from home, three days later. Her body was partly destroyed by crabs and other fish and he identified her by her ring, which he recovered. He buried her

11

there. He was in the marsh in an area where only a good cow pony could carry him. This event had such an effect upon my father, who was a very sensitive person, that he told my mother when they married that that was the last funeral to which he ever intended to go. He almost kept that promise to himself, because I never remember my father attending a funeral, except that of his mother and my mother. The reason at the time, I did not know. This is just one incident which illustrates the hardships under which the people lived three-quarters of a century ago. I am not saying that it was only the people of this area who were confronted with such tragedies; entire families were wiped out by Indians further west.

CHAPTER TWO

THE HOMESTEADERS

I had a brother and two sisters. Eleric Webb McCall was born in 1890 and died in 1971, in Denton, Texas, where he then resided with his wife of 53 years, Julia Medlin McCall. Alice McCall was born in 1893 at Sabine Pass, has never married and still resides at the old home of my parents in Hamshire, Texas. She is a remarkable person and is assisting me in this work. I may devote some further space to her later in this narrative. My youngest sister, who was six years younger than myself, Lovie McCall, married Otto Fischer; both are deceased. She was blessed with four children, all of whom are married and doing well.

At some period of time prior to my father's marriage, the exact time I do not know, he was engaged in the butcher business in partnership with his father, John McCall, and other early settlers. This was probably a very lucrative business, but for reasons which I will probably relate in a subsequent chapter, my father withdrew from this business and for several years was engaged as a tenant farmer, which was a very hard way to make a living in Sabine Pass at that time. This butcher business apparently paid very well because, prior to the storm of 1886, Sabine Pass was a thriving town and Texans have always consumed a lot of beef. In addition to the local market, these men had become very adept in the art of pickling beef and were furnishing a great deal of pickled beef to the ships which came to Sabine Pass. The methods of refrigeration that we now have were unknown at that time and the seagoing vessels had to have meat that would keep on their voyages.

I remember, as a small child, seeing many times on a living room table in my grandmother's living room, a silver medal which had been given to my grandfather, John McCall, by the United States government, certifying the excellent quality of the pickled beef which he furnished to the government vessels. The knowledge which my father gained in handling the various kinds of meat, and preserving them for human consumption was very valuable and had a lot to do with our survival in later years.

When my older brother and I were born, my father was a tenant farmer on what was known as the "Old Johnson Place" about two miles west of the old town of Sabine Pass. When my first sister was born, he was a tenant farmer on what was known as the "Frank Keith Place" on the back ridge. The farming at Sabine Pass in those days consisted of raising food for human and animal consumption, such as melons and all types of vegetables, which found some market in the town of Sabine Pass. In addition they had begun to raise long-staple cotton which had become valuable.

My grandfather, W. J. Webb, was also a small tenant farmer in the area. Living with him were his three teen-aged boys and his third daughter, Lovie Webb, mentioned above. My grandfather realized that there was very little opportunity for his family or the family of his married daughter, my mother, to ever acquire any property at Sabine Pass. He learned that in 1895, the State of Texas was opening up for homesteaders an area in the western part of Jefferson County and eastern part of Chambers County. He persuaded my father to migrate with him and acquire land. While the distance we traveled from our former home to where I now live at Hamshire, Texas was not very great, this was wild country in 1895. The only way to survive was to actually wrestle a living from the soil and my father, because of his background and natural industry, was well equipped to do that. Many of the 1895 homesteaders did not make it.

As anyone familiar with Texas history knows, prior to the Texas Revolution in 1836, Texas belonged to Mexico, and for many years the Mexican government desired that Texas be settled by persons from the eastern states. Texas was a vast wilderness and was of little value to the Mexican government in its then existing condition. Everyone is familiar with the history of Moses and Stephen Austin. Moses Austin, who was in the real estate business, perhaps in Missouri, made a trip to Mexico City and made a deal with the Mexican government which authorized him to bring thousands of settlers from the States into Texas. As the story goes, he was subjected to severe hardships and exposure on the trip to Mexico and back and died. His son, Stephen Austin, who was then in a law school in New Orleans, took up the work and brought thousands of settlers to South Central Texas.

The center of these settlements was old Washington-on-the-Brazos and Columbus, Texas. In addition, there were many other persons that had simi-

14

lar contracts with the Mexican government on a smaller scale and many settlements resulted from the immigration. The extreme southeast portion of Texas had a little different background. There were many persons, mostly from the States and from Mexico, who acquired land grants in this area of Texas. The seat of government was in Nacogdoches and anyone desiring to settle in Texas came to Nacogdoches, declared his citizenship and requested a land grant. He was given permission to select the land which was surveyed and, later, he was issued a grant from the Mexican government. These grants were mostly in "leagues" of land, which is an area three miles square, embracing nine sections of 640 acres each. For this narrative the important grants are those that existed in the western part of Jefferson County and the eastern part of Chambers County. The league grants in the western part of Jefferson County were the Smith League, the west line of which was approximately two miles east of Hamshire, the David Burrell League, which was immediately east and northeast of the Smith League, the Chirino League, which was north of the David Burrell League, the J. C. Lawhon League, which adjoined the Chirino League on the northwest, the McFarland League, which was near Nome, Texas, and the Vacocu League, the north line of which is about a mile and a half south of Hamshire. The four leagues which are important in the eastern part of Chambers County are the J. M. Duran League, the James Hoggatt League, the E. Lopez League and the Valmore League. They were in an almost exact square involving an area of six square miles. The Valmore and Lopez Leagues are partly in Jefferson and partly in Chambers County. The east line of the Valmore League is about a mile and a half west of Hamshire. The west line of the Hoggatt and Duran Leagues is approximately two miles west of Winnie. The town of Winnie is entirely within the Hoggatt League. All of these grants that were made prior to the revolution were validated when Texas became a Republic and the titles to the grantees and their subsequent grantees were made good.

Prior to 1895, a company was organized to build a railroad from Beaumont to Galveston. In fact, the original plan was to go further north. It was called the Gulf and Interstate Railroad. This project was begun by three men: Fox Winnie, the man for whom the town was named, Buffalo Jones and Shanghai Pierce. I do not know the background of Winnie or Buffalo Jones, but anyone familiar with the history of the cattle barons of Texas has some knowledge of Shanghai Pierce.

My grandfather, W. J. Webb, learned two things. First, that the railroad was going to be built and second, that the State of Texas had opened up for homesteads all of the sections lying between the various Spanish grants in the western portion of Jefferson and the northeastern portion of Chambers

County. Any citizen of Texas could acquire one of these sections by living on it three years and paying $3.00 per acre for what was called "agricultural sections," and $2.50 per acre for what was called "grazing sections". The homesteader had 40 years within which to pay the State. I recall that my father's annual payment was $58.00 per year and I also recall, very distinctly, what a hard time my mother had saving nickels and dimes that came into her hands so that she would have the $58.00 to pay each year. Money was a very scarce item in those days.

My grandfather ascertained the route of the railroad and he selected Section 136, because the railroad was coming through that section and he had dreams of building a town. In fact, he did lay out originally what was called the townsite of Hamshire and I believe that he sold two lots during his lifetime. He did not live to see Hamshire develop to any great extent. There was organized in Galveston, a Winnie Townsite Company, which was a subsidiary of the Gulf and Interstate Railroad Company. The town of Winnie was laid out in lots which were 25 or 50 feet wide and there were also one-acre tracts laid out on the north, west and south of the townsite. The rest of the league was cut up in 10 and 20-acre tracts. I have often wondered how Fox Winnie, a manager of a townsite development, expected to sell these small tracts at that period of time when the only way a living could be made for a family was by raising cattle, and a league of land, or 5,760 acres, was about the minimum acreage required to make it possible. It was only after beginning this narrative that the probable reason dawned upon me. (See the following chapter on Providence rice.)

Fox Winnie probably heard about the rice being grown in Jefferson County and knew of the rice paddies of China and had visions of small rice farms on his 10 and 20-acre tracts; but, as will be seen in the following chapter, this was a false vision. He sold a good many lots in the townsite, but very few 10 and 20-acre tracts and these were all to people who came from the north and knew nothing of the cattle business or the rice business. All of the Hoggatt and Duran Leagues, except the townsite, were in 10 and 20-acre tracts and went by the name of Winnie Suburbs. During the period of time from 1895 to 1900, practically every section which was submitted for homesteaders was taken up and quite a little town grew up in Winnie.

CHAPTER THREE

PROVIDENCE RICE

Many years prior to 1895, there were settlers from Louisiana in the western part of Jefferson County, Texas—some in the Smith League, the Burrell League, the Chirino League and the Lawhon League, and others on smaller Spanish grants. The settlers had been here for many years and I do not know how long ago the French settlements started, but I am sure it was prior to the Civil War and possibly prior to the Texas Revolution. I know some of these houses were old homes when we came here in 1895. Some of these French people had planted rice in some of the sloughs and low land and, because of several wet summers, the rice did well. It must be understood that there were no canals in those days and no irrigation systems other than damming a slough, planting the rice below the dam and letting the water flow through the rice field when needed. These small tracts of rice had made such yields that many people were attracted to the area and homesteaded the land, not knowing that very little of the land was adaptable to rice by that kind of irrigation even in wet years. I think the term "Providence rice" originated from the idea that the farmer would plant his rice and depend upon an act of Providence to send him rain.   Section 136, which was homesteaded by my father and grandfather, had a slough running through it which embraced about 40 acres of low land. In the spring of 1896, my father placed a dam across the slough along the north line of the section which trapped the rain waters of the winter and early spring, and planted 40 acres of rice. When the rice needed water he could open the dam and irrigate by gravity. There happened to be a wet spring and plenty of water and he made a tremendous crop on the small tract in 1896. I remember vaguely the crude methods used

17

in harvesting. He had no combine nor rice binder. Most of the rice was cut with a scythe and the bundles tied by hand. Everything looked good. He planted a crop the same way in 1897, but it did not rain and his rice has not come up yet. That was the end of Providence rice so far as we were concerned and, in fact, because of the dry year in 1897 the growing of Providence rice was abandoned.

We went back to Sabine Pass and stayed until 1902, and when we came back Winnie was a ghost town. There were only two homes occupied—one by the man who pumped water for the railroad and the other by the postmaster. I do not think there were over eight or ten of the homesteaders left in the Winnie-Hamshire area. There was an old shack on practically every section which had been abandoned and, as I recall, riding over the prairie after cattle in those days, most of the shacks were being used by cattle as a refuge from cold weather and mosquitoes. Winnie had been quite a little town. I was too young to remember its size, but I do know that when we returned in 1902 there were probably 20 vacant houses.

I know that Winnie had a church in 1896 because I well remember an incident when we were going to church in a two-horse wagon from our home at Hamshire, five miles away, one Sunday morning. My parents were very devout Baptists and would not miss church and Sunday school if it were at all possible to attend. Our only means of transportation in those days was either by horseback or a two-horse wagon. We had no buggy, so we used a two-horse wagon to carry us to church and Sunday school.

My father was a very good hand at building wagon beds. These are sometimes referred to as wagon boxes, which of course is a box-like structure approximately four feet wide, one foot deep and perhaps ten feet in length, depending upon the length of the wagon. These wagon boxes were built from cypress wood and my father built them very well so that any material hauled in the wagon would not leak out. The one we were using that Sunday was too well built because it had no cracks through which water could drain. The wagon bed was set on the running gear of the wagon and not attached. It was held down by the weight of the box and the load on the wagon. However, there were no means to prevent it from going upward if conditions were right. In fact, we had often removed the box entirely when we hauled lumber and such articles on the wagon's frame.

There was no road to Winnie, just a trail across the prairie, and no bridges across the creeks. The slough which ran through our section developed into quite a little creek just below our south section line and there was a crossing, not a bridge, but a place where the banks were worn down on each side so that a wagon could be pulled in and out. On this Sunday morning, there had

18

been quite a rain and the creek was a little higher than Dad realized and when he drove the team of horses into the creek with my mother and three children in the wagon box, the box floated with all of us on it. The horses and wagon frame came out on the other side, leaving us in midstream. Dad rescued us safely, but we did not get to church. However, we were baptized in a most unconventional manner!

CHAPTER FOUR

GEORGE WASHINGTON AND THE CHERRY TREE

A story of the events which occurred in 1895, which attempts to show the primitive method of travel and the undeveloped condition of the area at that time, would not be complete without some reference to our trip from Sabine Pass to Hamshire.

All of the farming tools, the furniture, coops of chickens, and family were loaded on two wagons and the cattle were driven. This trip began at Sabine Pass and went west along the Gulf of Mexico beach to High Island. There was no passenger service and no freight service; only a work train used the tracks. Somehow, my father or my grandfather negotiated with the construction people and as a result all the household goods, the plows, the furniture, and my mother and three children were loaded on a flatcar. Everything was then covered with a tarpaulin and the flatcar pulled by the work train to Hamshire. The horses and cattle were driven through the prairie. Imagine my mother's discomfort and anxiety traveling on a flatcar with three children and all her possessions, through an all-day rain covered with a tarpaulin. The work train had other cars and some switching was necessary between High Island and Hamshire. The methods used for switching cars was not designed for passengers. When cars were added to the train, the cars in route were released at high speeds and allowed to collide with the cars to be picked up. This technique was called a "flying switch". My uncle, John Webb, who was with my mother on the flatcar, observing her fright, in an abortive attempt to alleviate her anxiety said, "Don't worry, Sue, we have only one more flying switch to make." My grandfather, with his family, had preceded us by a few weeks and had built a four-room house with split pine shingles. My earliest recollection, at three years of age, was of arriving just as the sun went down and the rain had stopped. There was nothing in Hamshire at that time but that shack. We were west of the old French settlement and there was nothing between our house and the town of Winnie, which had just begun to grow.

This little shack was very primitive, built of rough pine lumber and called a box house. That meant the sides were made of 12-inch rough pine boards placed upright and the cracks between them were covered by 1 x 4 inch rough pine strips. Of course, inside plumbing was unheard of in those days. I think those conditions can be best illustrated by the following story which was told to me as something resembling the truth.

An early settler (whose name is withheld) settled just before the turn of the century in western Chambers County and built his home on the high bank of the Trinity River. The bathroom, (which was in those days called a "privy") was constructed in this manner: two large logs were found; one end of both was placed on the bank and the other ends extended out over the river where the water was deep; that end of the two logs was supported by a long pole, one end of which was driven into the river bottom with the top end extending above the logs. The "useful" part of the structure was far out over the river and was reached from the land by a sort of pier created with boards nailed on top of the logs between the land and the main structure. This was good from a sanitary standpoint, but hard on the women in the family when the weather was bad.

The members of this family consisted of the rancher, his wife and two sons. As the years passed, the rancher and his wife advanced in age and the two boys, who at the time of this incident were in their late teens, had been away at school and had learned that some people in other parts of the country had modern plumbing facilities in their homes. By this time, the rancher's economic condition had greatly improved. The price of steers had increased from $5.00 per head, to $15.00 per head and then to $25.00 per head.

The oldest son, being concerned about his mother's health and comfort, said to his father, "Now Dad, you can well afford to put modern plumbing in the home so mother will not have to go out in all kinds of weather." The father's answer was that this was good enough for his parents back in Mississippi and always had been good enough for him and that he was not going to do anything about it. This displeased the son, so one afternoon when the boy, who had been out on the prairie working cattle, rode in for a sandwich and seeing that his father's favorite saddle horse was not in sight and his mother's buggy was gone, said to himself, "Now is a good time to fix that damn thing once and for all!" So he rode up to the bank of the river, threw a

21

loop of his rope on that part of the supporting pole which stuck up above the timber, tied the other end of the rope to his saddle pommel and put spurs to his very stout cow pony. The result was that the whole structure collapsed and went downstream. The boy went back to his work with the cattle feeling he had done a good deed.

This was before corporal punishment of children was abandoned. About sundown that evening, the boy came riding up to the ranch house and saw the old man sitting on the porch with a cow whip in his hand. The boy said to himself, "Somehow the old man knows what I did and is going to give me a whipping." The boy had read the story of George Washington and how, when a child, George had cut down his father's favorite cherry tree, and George's father did not punish him because George admitted the truth. He said to himself, "I will try that on the old man." He rode up to the porch. The old man said, "Come here boy. I am going to whip you. Why did you dump that thing in the river?" The boy said, "Yes, Dad, I did it. I am telling you the truth and you should be just as considerate as George Washington's father was when George admitted cutting down the cherry tree." The old man an-answered, "This is altogether different. When George Washington cut down that cherry tree, his father wasn't *in* it!"

CHAPTER FIVE

WHEN THE ANTS GOT OUR DINNER

We gave up rice farming and went back to Sabine Pass in the year 1897. There was no way in the world to eke out a living in Hamshire at that time. Providence rice had failed. There was no market for other farm crops and no opportunity to secure wages for any kind of labor. My father and mother decided to go back to Sabine Pass on a visit and perhaps find there some means to support the family. He hitched up the two-horse wagon and drove to Sabine Pass by way of Beaumont. In those days when people traveled, the housewives prepared a lot of good food to take along and as I recall, my mother had cooked a lot of things, including fried chicken and a cake. I do not recall ever getting enough of her fried chicken or cake in those days. We reached the bridge on Taylor's Bayou, where Port Arthur is now, about noon and it was very warm weather. My father decided to camp there and let the horses rest and eat our lunch before proceeding on to Sabine Pass, ten miles further south. As I recall, there were three houses in what is now Port Arthur. There were several shade trees on the bank of the bayou, so it was decided to unhitch the horses, feed them, and let them rest. We could all lie down and take a little nap in the shade of the trees before we ate our lunch. It so happened that the lunch was taken out of the wagon and put at the trunk of a tree in the shade while we all took a nap. When we awoke, some half hour or so later, it was discovered that the lunch had been put on top of an ant bed and the entire lunch was covered with ants. The cake and the chicken and everything else was simply a mass of ants, so we had nothing to eat and went on to Sabine Pass without food. Of course, we were a bunch of hungry kids when we got to my grandmother's at Sabine Pass late that afternoon.

During our absence of two years from Sabine Pass, many changes had taken place. The Kountze brothers from New York, who acquired a vast area of timber land in Southeast Texas and for whom the town of Kountze was named, had also acquired a vast amount of land at Sabine Pass and were building a town two miles below the old town of Sabine Pass called Newtown. The intention was to have a shipping port there for the shipping of lumber from East Texas. There was a lot of building going on and, since my father was a fairly good carpenter, he went to work with his uncle, Jack Garner, as a carpenter for Kountze Brothers. Among other jobs he had was the building of a little two-room house on a large tract of land, which Kountze had acquired, about a mile out of the town of old Sabine Pass. After the house was completed, we moved into it as a tenant of Mr. Kountze and finally leased a pasture from Kountze. My father, within a few months, started a little dairy.

There was a good market for milk in Newtown, which was building very fast. My father had some cattle and he accumulated from his herd about twelve cows which were fairly good milk cows and built a barn. I recall that the barn had a wooden floor and had stalls for twelve cows, six on each side. We did not have to comply with all the sanitary conditions that are mandatory now. He would get up in the morning at four o'clock and milk the cows, strain and cool the milk, and carry it to town with a one-horse rig in two ten-gallon cans. When Dad would drive down the street he would ring a bell and the housewives would come out with a pitcher. He would draw a quart, two quarts or whatever amount they wanted to buy, from the faucet on the can and pour it into their containers. Dad did fairly well in the milk business in a small way, but I think that was partly due to the fact that he did not have to hire any labor.

When I was seven years of age and my brother nine, we took turns with the milking; I would get up one morning and help my father milk and my brother would get up the next morning. My father put the six easiest cows to milk on one side for my brother and me to milk, and the ones that were hard to milk on the other side for him to milk. So it was my job every other morning to get up at four o'clock and milk six cows, beginning when I was seven years of age. When these cows were milked and the milk cooled and sent to town, we would go back to bed and sleep until my mother woke us up for a late breakfast. After breakfast it was our duty to turn the cows into the pasture, clean out the barn and place some feed in the troughs for evening milking. In addition we did whatever other jobs were to be done around the farm until four o'clock when the milking process would start again.

Dad did not peddle milk on Sundays, so we had a lot of extra milk from which my mother made country butter and another product which I'll never forget. On Saturday evening, my father would always bring home ice, salt, and other material for making ice cream. We had a big two-gallon freezer, and on Sundays we made the surplus milk up into ice cream, which was the best ice cream I have ever eaten in my life. On Sunday morning, we would go to Sunday school and church in the same one-horse rig from which my father peddled milk on weekdays. This wagon was pulled by an old bay horse, "Dick", a very faithful work and saddle horse for many years.

Newtown, at Sabine, was prosperous for a few years while under construction but it never amounted to much. Kountze never realized his dream to make Sabine a main port; Stillwell and others started the town of Port Arthur. When we came back to Hamshire from Sabine Pass in 1902, five years after the prolonged visit, I remember very well that Port Arthur was a beautiful little town; everything was new, and freshly painted and I thought it was the prettiest sight I'd ever seen. Sabine was dying and Port Arthur was growing. The Port Arthur ship channel, from Sabine Pass, was either being built or had been built by the government, making Port Arthur a deep-water port. Although my father was doing well with his small dairy and making a good living for his family, circumstances occurred which caused him to return to Hamshire.

CHAPTER SIX

THE RICE INDUSTRY IMPROVES

Hundreds of cattle which were unprotected in the marshes and prairies of Sabine Pass died as a result of a prolonged siege of mosquitoes and anthrax. I think it was this, the 1900 storm and its aftermath, and the fact that Sabine Pass was dying that caused my father to decide to leave Sabine Pass permanently. It was not until the first few days of August, 1902, that he finally managed to get away. We came back in the same two-horse wagon that had brought us to Sabine Pass five years before, traveling by way of Port Arthur and Beaumont. We spent the night in Beaumont. The next morning when we went to leave, the wagon, which by then had gotten quite old, broke down on Railroad Avenue while crossing the railroad track. Railroad Avenue was not paved in those days. Dad unhitched the team from the wagon and went to the Caffall Carriage Company and bought a new wagon. He also bought a new mowing machine because of news from our uncles that prairie grass was very good on the Hamshire section.

In those days thousands of acres of the prairie here were covered with what was called South Texas prairie grass which made a very good quality of hay. South Texas prairie grass did not have the strongest elements of animal food, but was good clean hay and grew luxuriantly. We came back on the 6th day of August, 1902, and began making hay for market.

Haymaking in those days was much different from now. The mowing machine was pulled by two horses and cut a five-foot swath. The hay was raked up in windrows with a hay rake and from there dragged to the baler by a bull rake, which was made of wood. There was no such thing as a power baler at that time; the baler was powered by a horse. The South Texas prai-

26

rie hay dried very easily. On a good, hot, summer day you could mow it in the early morning, rake it in early afternoon and bale it before night. Three men and a boy, working hard, could bale a hundred bales or about three tons in one afternoon. We loaded the hay on boxcars at Hamshire and shipped it to Beaumont, where it brought $7.00 a ton. This was not a lot of money but it was a way to exist until we could get a farming operation started. In the meantime, rice farming had undergone a change. Our land was not adapted to the new methods of irrigation so we undertook to make our living by what was called high-land farming.

As I continue this narrative of my early life, it may be well to pause and give an account of the changes in the rice industry from 1896 to 1976. The rice industry in our area is second only to the oil industry and has made a great contribution to the development of the country and its inhabitants. Already I have given an account of my experience with Providence rice which depended entirely upon rainfall which was not always plentiful. It is interesting to note the phenomenal changes which have taken place from the standpoint of operation and production since I first began working as a $1.00 a day laborer in the rice fields. In the early years of this century there were, of course, no combines, trucks or tractors; power was supplied primarily by mules. They were heavy Missouri mules which were imported for rice farming and were much better adapted to the muddy rice fields than horses.

For an economical farm, the proper planting unit was about 100 acres per year. Such land was valued at about $15 per acre. The necessary equipment consisted of five large mules, a gang plow, a disk, a harrow, a drill and a binder. The total investment, including the land, would be about $4,000. A good crop was about 10 barrels per acre and a barrel sold for about $3.00.

Now, under present farming methods, an economical unit for planting is about 225 acres which would have a market value of about $400 per acre. Necessary equipment consists of two tractors, two heavy disk plows, a combine and a "doodle bug", which conveys the rice from the combine to the road. Also a large truck is needed to haul the rice from the farm to the mill or dryer. At present costs for land and machinery, an investment of about $140,000 is necessary.

Under conditions which prevailed in 1908, since everything the farmer had to have was inexpensive, he could exist on $30 per acre of gross income. Now in 1976, the best of rice farmers cannot produce a crop of less than $350 per acre. Since the selling price is approximately $15 per barrel, if he yields less than 30 barrels per acre there will be no return on his investment.

During our absence from Hamshire several families had moved into what was called the Stringtown country. They had their homes on sections which they had taken up on Mayhaw Bayou and the south prong of Taylor's Bayou. The Stringtown community consisted of the following families: George Gill, Charlie Wilber, C. Q. Taylor, a man by the name of File, Charlie Groves, B. R. Curtis, and the Garland family. There may have been one or two others which I do not recall at this time. These people had chosen sections of land on the bayous further downstream from our home, where there was available water which could be pumped from the stream. The irrigation of rice in those days was a very crude arrangement. The farmer would build the canal from the bayou to his field using mules, fresno scrapers and a lot of handwork. On the bayou, he would set a pump powered by a steam engine he fueled with mayhaw and hoghaw wood, which grew abundantly along the bayous. This was a hard way to make a living, but these families survived and some did quite well. By that time every rice farmer had a binder which was drawn by five horses or mules and which cut the rice and tied it in bundles. There was a bundle carrier on the rear end of the binder and when about half a dozen bundles accumulated, the binder operator would dump the bundles in piles. The bundles had to be picked up by the shocking crew, which picked them up and put the bundles in shocks, which was a little stack comprising about two dozen bundles. They had to be put up carefully or they would fall down in the mud. Sometimes the shocking was done in mud and water about a foot deep and was miserable, hard work. We had to wear gloves or the roughness of the rice would make our fingers bleed. After the rice was cured in the shocks for about two weeks it was thrashed.

When I first began to work the rice harvest in my early teens, the thrashing machines were hand fed. The wagons from the field would come up on each side of the separator, the wagon driver would pitch the bundle on a platform and a boy would stand there with a pocket knife to cut the bands and shove the bundle over to the man in the center who was feeding it into the cylinders. The farmer would always try to set the separator in such a way that the wind would be blowing from the feeding crew into the separator, but the wind would shift and the dust would fog out; it was almost unbearable. If there was a wet fall and they could not get into the fields to harvest and it continued to rain, sometime the butts, that is the lower end of the bundle, would rot. I remember many times when we had to throw the bundles off on the ground at the separator and chop the wet ends off with a broadaxe before they could be put in the separator.

A full thrashing crew at that time was about 21 men consisting of 12 wagons with their drivers, about 6 men in the field pitching the bundles up to the wagons, 2 sack draggers who dragged the sacks away from the separators as they were filled, and a sack sewer. The separators were powered with a stationary steam engine. When time came to move from one location to another, all of the mules in the field had to be hitched to the front end of the separator in order to change it to a new location. Another team was required to haul wood and water to the boiler. Today with the modern combines, three men comprise a harvest crew and no one touches anything except a steering wheel, a lever or a starter switch.

When I was in my teens, ten sacks of rice was considered a good crop. When I worked one fall in the rice harvest for the Kennesons on what is called the Will Denny Farm, which had been farmed for many years at that time and the land considered worn out, they made four sacks to the acre. Right across the road my brother worked for Frank Crowley, who was farming a piece of sod and made fourteen sacks to the acre. People came to see such a good crop. I have seen the two fields make thirty barrels to the acre side by side in recent years under modern farming conditions.

The reader may wonder why farms which were considered worn out 65 or 70 years ago are now capable of producing nearly ten times as much rice. This is attributed to scientific methods. For instance, with heavy machinery, the land is prepared better, making irrigation more uniform. In addition, the farmers have learned to use proper fertilizers and proper quantities of each. The most significant advance is the remarkable development of herbicides which destroy the grass and weeds and do not injure the rice.

In the early days, as soon as the farmer harvested his rice in the fall, he started plowing for the next spring. He had to plow in all kinds of weather: cold, wet or dry. If something were to happen, requiring the present generation of rice farmers to revert to production of rice by the old method, I assure you there would be no surplus of either rice or rice farmers.

CHAPTER SEVEN

RETURN TO THE OLD HOMESTEAD

In the previous chapter, I digressed from the general narrative of the family history, which I left with our return to Hamshire, Texas in 1902.

When we returned to the old place, after five years' absence, it was in bad need of repair; but my father, with the help of my mother and my older brother, then twelve years old, and what help I could give, then ten years of age, set about to make a living from the soil. A part of the section of land was especially adapted to the growing of high land crops. We did not at that time have enough cattle, given the low price of steers, to produce a living income.

After the hay season of 1902 was over, my father planted a fall garden, but the place had become so overrun with cottontail rabbits that soon they ate up the garden. Turning disaster into profit, we built rabbit traps (which in itself required some skill) and literally lived on rabbits in the winter of 1902 and 1903. I will here state that an epicure who never tasted rabbit gravy and biscuits as my mother prepared them has missed something. By the spring of 1903, the rabbits being thinned out, our crop began to prosper. We first procured seed cane from a neighboring ranchman and planted our first crop. There was little change in life on the farm at Hamshire between 1902 until 1910. By hard work on the part of everyone and, as a result of my father's early training in the art of living from the soil, we were able to live with some degree of comfort. We had a sufficient number of work and saddle stock, which we had acquired from Mr. Arceneaux.

It might be proper at this point to give some history of the cattle business, and the men involved.

Our nearest neighbor was the Edgar Caruthers family. Edgar Caruthers was a fine old Frenchman who had migrated from Louisiana many years before we came. He was a good man, but a hard man. He did not have many cattle and supported his family much as my father did. His hardness was no doubt justified by the necessity of coping with ecological facts which existed and which pertained to our survival. As a teenager, I worked for Mr. Caruthers. We got along well together and I believe that association had something to do with my later "hang-up" on hard work and my unfortunate inability to relax.

There are descendants of Mr. Caruthers now living in the Hamshire community who are fine people. In meditating over the matter after all these years, I have come to the conclusion that, on the whole, these early settlers were a very high type of people.

I believe the next nearest neighbor was Louis Aubey, a fine old Frenchman, for whom I hoed corn. Mr. Aubey had about 200 head of cattle at the time and, with the crops he grew on his farm, was in a comfortable position. His place was remarkable. He always had a good crop of corn and, therefore, fat horses, a pen full of hogs and a lot of chickens and turkeys. His wife was a fine woman and cousin to my paternal grandmother. They raised a fine family and have several descendants in the area now. One of his great-granddaughters, Brenda Webb, now works in the law office for my son and me, and a better woman I have never known.

I always feel a pang of guilt when I think of the incident when I shot Mr. Aubey's dog. In about the year 1904, when I was about 12 years of age, Moise Johnson (a son-in-law of Mr. Arceneaux) ran a little country store about a quarter mile from my home. Mr. Johnson also was the postmaster and kept the Post Office in the back of the store. Mr. Aubey had a habit of driving his buggy to the Post Office and hitching his big, fat, sorrel buggy horse right against the steps to the store gallery. Afterwards, he would sit in the store and discuss the weather with the accumulated neighbors. Mr. Aubey had a very faithful bulldog which always laid under the buggy at all times while Mr. Aubey was away from it. I had heard Moise Johnson say to Mr. Aubey, "Louis, if that dog ever bites me, I'm going to kill him." Mr. Aubey said, "Moise, that dog is not going to bother you if you don't mess with my buggy." One day my mother sent me to the store for something. Mr. Aubey had hitched the buggy so close to the steps that when I stepped on the porch, the bulldog thought I was too close to the buggy. The first thing I knew, the dog had me by the leg. I kicked him off but was too bashful to complain to Mr. Aubey. While the dog had drawn only a little blood, I silently swore vengeance.

A few days later, my father butchered a steer and, as always when that happened, all of the dogs in the neighborhood smelled the blood and came around. I looked up and saw the Aubey bulldog in the bushes. Previously, my father had offered me 25¢ for each gopher I trapped on the farm because they were destroying the crops. I earned enough to buy a Stevens singleshot .22 rifle and had gotten to be a pretty good shot. I ran to the house and loaded my rifle. As I returned, the dog was running into the bushes. I took such aim as I could and shot. I heard the dog yelp, but did not know how badly I had hurt him or whether I had killed him.

I was scared. I knew Mr. "Louie", as we called him, thought a lot of his dog and feared he would find out that I shot him. I never mentioned the incident to anyone. About two days later, I was in the store and Mr. Louie came in and said "Moise, you shot my dog." Moise denied having shot the dog and Mr. Louie said "Yes you did, he came home the other day and was lying on the porch and someone had shot him. The bullet went in behind the ribs and lodged in his neck and every time he moves he yelps." Moise, who owned a .44 Winchester, said "Now look here, old man, I did not shoot your damn dog. If I had, the bullet would not have lodged in his neck. It would have gone all the way through him and hollered for more dog on the other side."

Of course, I said nothing, but went out of the store as quickly as possible. The dog got well, and both he and Mr. Louie have long since died of old age. Until this day, nobody but the dog and I ever knew who shot the dog or why.

CHAPTER EIGHT

GETTING OUR LIVING FROM THE SOIL

As mentioned, our land at Hamshire was not adaptable to rice farming as we had no creeks on our land from which water could be pumped. We had to figure out a way to make our living from the soil by high land farming. That consisted of raising sweet potatoes, Irish potatoes, sugarcane, watermelons and other marketable crops. We raised feed for our animals also. We simply had to live from the soil; there was no other source.

I think my father and mother realized it would be a hard life when they made the move. My mother was a fine, stoic woman and took the hardships with a smile, although she was a product of the old southern antebellum aristocracy. She made an excellent poor man's wife and a wonderful mother of her four children. I was ten years old when we came back to Hamshire; my brother was twelve; my oldest sister, eight and my youngest sister, Lovie, who was born at Sabine Pass, four. I remember my mother and father discussing the question of coming back to the farm and the possibility of making a living there. My mother said to my father, "We can make it now because the boys are big enough to work." And work we did.

Winnie, which was a thriving little village when we left in 1897, was a ghost town in 1902. Trains were making regular trips from Beaumont to Galveston. The town of Stowell had improved due to a rice canal being built from Anahuac eastward to near Stowell. A new kind of rice industry had sprung up. Water was pumped from what was then Turtle Bay (and is now Lake Anahuac) into the canal and across a very fine rice farming area in the central part of Chambers County. Among others who had moved to Stowell was the Ogden Family; L. G. Ogden ran a hardware store. There was also the

Sterett family, which operated a rather large general store. R. M. White had moved from his original home near Hankamer and built a nice home at Stowell, and many other persons had settled. I do not recall the population of Stowell in 1902, but it was a thriving little village.

Our section of land had some high, sandy ridges which were well adapted to what we called high land crops. However, high land farming was not a very lucrative way to make a living.

Cattle, being cheap, were the mainstay of a farmer's income and we did not have enough cattle to market. I think we had about a hundred head when we moved back to Hamshire in 1902. We left them in Sabine Pass and returned in the spring of 1903 to bring them to Hamshire. However, our section of land had high, sandy ridges which were adaptable to high-land crops.

High-land farming in those days consisted of raising corn for the stock; it was fed to the horses, hogs, and chickens. We found at first the only money crop was Irish potatoes and we later began to make cane syrup commercially. The growth of ribbon cane and making of syrup was quite a task in those days. Every old settler had a little patch of cane, in some instances not more than a quarter of an acre and some even less. The loamy land in the Hamshire area was well adapted to the growth of ribbon cane. The cane was very juicy and tender, not hard like the cane used for sugar making in Louisiana. The old-fashioned ribbon cane was so tender and had such sweet juice that in the fall of the year we children would go to the cane patch on Sundays to chew ribbon cane. We would drink the juice and spit out the dry pulp until the pile was so big we could hardly spit over it.

Most communities had a cane mill or, more properly, a syrup mill. Mr. Lovan Hamshire, the man for whom Hamshire was named, had a mill and ground cane for all the neighbors. I worked for him several falls when I was in my teens. About the year 1907 or 1908 my father bought the mill and moved it to our farm. We raised more cane than any of the other farmers and we became syrup makers for the whole community. The cost was either one-third of the syrup or sixteen cents per gallon. Small producers would bring their two or three wagon loads of cane to the mill. With the last load they would bring a barrel, a keg or whiskey jugs and, when the syrup was made, they would take it home. Every settler had a keg or barrel of syrup on the back porch with a molasses gate from which the housewife would draw the syrup for each meal. No one in this generation has ever tasted anything as good as properly made ribbon cane syrup and soda biscuits. The syrup had to be cooked just right. If the syrup was cooked too done, it would turn to sugar before it could be consumed; if it was not cooked enough, it would sour. If it turned to sugar in the barrel, the barrel would be opened by the farmer when the sugar had formed and the housewife would re-cook it; this had a very fine flavor, but not the same as the original syrup. Even if the syrup soured a little, it still had a very desirable, if unique, taste. My brother became an expert syrup maker in his late teens.

I want to give an account of the best meal I have ever eaten in my life. As mentioned, we had about a hundred head of cattle and, since they were raised on the coast country, my father realized they would never make the winters properly on the prairies where the grass was not as nutritious. So we would drive our cattle back to Sabine Pass for winter pasture every October, leaving them there all winter and bringing them back in the spring. They got the benefit of good winter range on the coast but missed the bad mosquito swarms of the summer. My brother and I started making these trips with my father when I was about eleven years old. This required getting in the saddle about four in the morning and riding until nine or ten at night. We usually took the cattle through what we called "the gap." That route was about forty-five miles. Sometimes we did not make it in a day and would have to camp on the way. Finally we started going through the Arceneaux ranch and crossing Salt Bayou about five miles below Big Hill at the mouth of Fence Lake. The distance was shorter, but the trip more rugged and hazardous because the crossing at Salt Bayou and Salt Bayou Marsh required swimming the bayou when the water was high and wading when the water was low.

One fall, I think it was about 1906, we had driven the cattle to Sabine Pass around "the gap", but Dad decided to return by way of the short route and cross Salt Bayou at Fence Lake. We left Sabine Pass about daylight and would have made it early, but we found the crossing of Salt Bayou very difficult and had a hard time getting our horses across. About four o'clock in the afternoon we arrived at the house where the Arceneaux ranch had its headquarters. They had a man working for them whose job it was to look after the cattle and repair the fences. He was a bachelor whom we called Dutch Joe and was quite a character. He very seldom had company and was awfully happy to see us, insisting we stop and eat which was exactly what we needed. You can imagine how hungry a fourteen year old boy could be after eating an early breakfast and having been in the saddle until four in the afternoon. Dutch Joe had not been to town for supplies for some time and the only thing he had to offer us was biscuits and cane syrup. He had a big ranch bakepan about two feet square, and really knew how to make soda biscuits! He had been to town some time before and bought a gallon of cane syrup. I'm sure it was made at our mill, but the syrup had soured to the extent that if you poured it in the plate it would foam slightly. Now I have eaten at many good eating places; the Waldorf-Astoria in New York, the famous cafes in

Boston, the Windsor Hotel in Montreal, the famous eating places in Philadelphia, the French Quarter in New Orleans, Fisherman's Wharf in San Francisco and many others, yet I can say honestly that the best meal I have eaten in my life was the soda biscuits and sour cane syrup served to us by Dutch Joe on the Arceneaux Ranch.

Cane was a dependable crop in the early nineteen hundreds. Some families had very little to eat except biscuits or cornbread and cane syrup. Though it may seem so, it really was not a poor diet. I want to discuss the process of raising this cane and converting it into syrup, which for some was a life-sustaining commodity.

First the cane had to be grown. Stalks for seed were cut in the fall before any frost occurred and before the harvest for syrup making. The eyes for next year's growth were found at the joints of the cane stalk. The stalks to be used for seed were cut full length. With leaves left on, they were bedded on the ground and covered with dirt. This method allowed the cane to retain its moisture and prevented frost damage.

About the latter part of February, these stalks were stripped of their leaves and planted by laying them end to end in a furrow and covered with soil. If conditions are right and the eyes are not injured, each eye will make a new stalk, which will begin growing about the first of April. Later, suckers will appear. Such planting will produce approximately 20 tons per acre yielding 400 gallons of syrup. Of course, this was a good crop; the average was perhaps about 240 gallons per acre.

This crop of cane had to be cared for from planting time until harvest in November. The harvesting in those days was all done by hand. After stripping the leaves, each stalk was topped and cut with a cane knife and hauled to the mill in a two-horse wagon.

The mill which pressed the raw juice from the cane as it came from the field consisted of three rollers. One was about 15 inches in diameter and about 12 inches tall. The two smaller rollers were about 8 inches in diameter and the same height as the larger one. The shafts of all three, which were in an upright position, were set in bearings both at the top and bottom. The shaft of the big roller, however, extended about 18 inches above the top of the bearing case. A 20-foot wooden beam was attached to the top of this shaft. The beam sloped downward until the lower end was about three feet from the ground and two horses were hitched to this end. As they pulled forward, they traveled in a circle of about 40 feet in diameter. As the horses pulled the beam, the rollers turned toward each other. The small roller, nearest to the man who fed the cane into the mill, was set a half inch from the larger roller. This space allowed the small end of the cane to be inserted between the rollers. The second small roller was near enough to catch the cane into its one-quarter inch opening. As the beam rotated and the stalks were fed into the rollers, the juice was pressed out, caught in a trough under the rollers and drained into a large bucket with a rubber hose in the bottom of it. The hose sloped downward and was buried under the ground and extended to a large wooden trough in the cooking house where the syrup making began.

When the cane was brought in from the field, it was piled in long ricks on the ground, which, of course, had to be outside of the circle where the horses tread. Sometimes there would be as much as 100 tons of cane piled there when the season began. All of the cane (a day's run being about 5 tons) had to be carried in the arms of the worker from the piles and placed in a rack attached to the mill so that the man feeding the mill could reach each stalk quickly. As the crushed cane came from between the rollers on the other side of the mill opposite the man feeding the rollers, it had to be taken outside the horses' circle. This person was known as the "feeder helper". I was it. Another 5 tons (less the weight of the juice) had to be moved quite a distance in the course of a day. Both feeder and helper had to time their trips to and from the mill so as not to interfere with the continuous circling of the horses.

The other equipment located in the cooking shed about 30 feet from the mill was a furnace, or fire box, which was constructed of brick and iron. The fire box was about 6 feet wide, 4 feet high, and 6 feet long. It would take about an eighth of a cord of wood at a time. Two brick walls led from each side of the fire box about 20 feet in length on which the cooking pan rested. At the rear was a smoke stack about 20 feet high. This allowed the heat from the fire box to go under the full length of the pan and through the smoke stack. The least heat was at the rear of the pan where the raw juice entered and the cooking process began. The juice passed through six sections in the pan and the sufficiently cooked syrup was taken off in the last section nearest the fire box.

As the juice was passing from one section to the other and starting to boil, all foreign substances rose to the surface and were skimmed off with a "skimmer". This operation was constant during the cooking process. When the cooking juice reached the final stage there would not be a particle of foreign substance and the syrup would be perfectly clear.

There was nothing added to the cane juice to prevent it from souring or turning to sugar. The syrup maker had to be so alert to the consistency of the syrup as it boiled that he knew exactly when to remove it from the heat.

In our case, the mill was not quite large enough to utilize the full capacity of the cooking facilities. Therefore, the mill had to be started at four a.m. to produce enough juice to justify starting the fire at 6 a.m. The mill would be stopped at 8 p.m. It took the workers an additional two hours to take care of the horses and wash and clean the mill. Thus the working hours were from 4 a.m. until 10 p.m. each weekday with neither the mill operators nor the cooking crew shutting down during these 18 hours.

When breakfast time came, the one who carried the cane and removed the crushed stalks (me) had to work fast, fill the rack full, go to breakfast and eat quickly. (What a breakfast we had! My mother was an excellent cook.) When I returned the rack was empty and the crushed cane had made a huge pile. This condition had to be hurriedly corrected so that the feeder man could go to breakfast. The same steps were repeated at noon and again at suppertime. The other six hours of the 24 were for sleep—and what a sleep! Who can describe the satisfaction of those six hours?

The mill ran only six days each week. We slept nearly the whole day Sunday. Four men, a boy (if such workmen could be called boys), two horses, the use of a cord of wood and 10,000 pounds of cane could, by working 18 hours, produce 100 gallons of fine cane syrup. For our own syrup, produced from the cane we raised, there was a ready market at fifty cents per gallon. For that which we made for the neighbors, we were paid sixteen cents per gallon as mentioned.

I am relating all of this to show a part of the methods by which we, seventy years ago, would wrest our means of survival from the soil. Perhaps the above will give some clue as to why I decided to become a lawyer. Later in this writing, more comment will be made as to the wisdom or lack of wisdom in that decision.

During the years from 1902 until 1920, we had to take our entire existence from the soil by these most primitive methods. Our equipment consisted of the horse, whose food we produced, a horse-drawn turning plow, a harrow, a sweep (sometimes called a Georgia stock), a hoe, and a shovel.

While I still say "The Good Old Times" are now, and I somehow envy the generation which has its youth in 1970's, I have a tinge of sorrow for this generation which never experienced the satisfaction of taking its life from the God-given earth. There is a bit of pity for the teenage youth who never, while following a walking plow barefooted in the spring, experienced the feel of cool, damp earth. There is no aroma so pleasant as that of newly plowed ground in the spring. And there is nothing so pleasing to taste as the flavor of soda biscuits, cane syrup, and homemade sausage at the end of a long day.

There is another matter worthy of thought when we contemplate the primitive way of life in those days. While I have never been considered overly religious, I must say that when your crop is your very subsistence and depends on good weather for growth (and the absence of unfavorable weather which could mean destruction) you are brought closer to the Supreme Being. You have this same feeling of dependence on something beyond human help when a member of your family is very sick and no doctor is available.

CHAPTER NINE

HURRICANES AND MOSQUITOES

The history of this area will not be complete without some reference to the periodical Gulf storms, hurricanes. Nowadays we hear a lot about them because every time one originates a thousand miles away we are kept posted as to its progress, but in those days the only warning the people had was the weather conditions preceding the storm, from which the old timers could pretty well tell when a storm was approaching. My father went through the storm of 1886; then came the storm of 1900. These were the two severe storms that struck the coast at Sabine Pass during his stay there. Of course, at the time of the storm in 1915, which was also very severe, we were at Hamshire. The place where we lived and operated the dairy in Sabine Pass was about a mile west of the old town and not in a high-ridge country. It was customary for the old timers at Sabine Pass to go to the homes on the highest part of the ridge when a storm was coming. In 1900, my father loaded our family in the two-horse wagon and we all went to the old Neil McGaffey home higher up on the ridge, about a mile and a half west of where we lived. I remember the old man, Neil McGaffey, very well. He was the son of John McGaffey referred to earlier. I remember old man McGaffey telling us during that night (he had probably a hundred refugees in his home at the time) how strong his house was built. When the storm was over and we got back home, the water had been four feet deep where we lived, but the house had not washed away and the barn was still standing. The cow pen was washed away but we did not lose any cattle. The south side had washed away and a carload of driftwood had drifted against the north fence and lodged there. In the middle of the cow pen a big cypress stump, probably four feet in diameter, had washed up. We never moved this stump because we had no tractor or team that was heavy enough to pull it. It remained there until the following summer. There was driftwood and debris all around the place. It took my father weeks and weeks to clean up before he could start his dairy business again.

The entire marsh in the Sabine Pass area was filled with salt water by the storm and, as mosquitoes do not breed in salt water, there were no mosquitoes in 1900. However, the rains in the year 1900 and 1901 were sufficient to wash the principal part of the salt out of the marshes, so that when the spring rains came in 1901 the conditions were exactly right for the breeding of mosquitoes.

We had no mosquitoes in the early spring nor any in the early summer. Just before sundown on the evening of July 15, 1901, a clear day, what seemed to be a cloud rose over the marshes. It was mosquitoes which had hatched in the marsh. By dark they hit the prairie and cattle were running up and down the field bellowing. My father got home about dark from his delivery of milk and, knowing that a fire would be more protection against the mosquitoes than smoke, set the big stump in the cow pen afire. The fire burned all night. The cattle circled around this fire for protection from the mosquitoes. As the mosquitoes flew near the fire, the heat killed them. The mosquitoes were so thick that when they dropped to the ground, as I recall, it was safe to say that the next morning you could have raked twenty bushels of dead mosquitoes from around the stump. Conditions were right for mosquitoes the remainder of the summer and the conditions that prevailed were almost unbearable and indescribable. We had to keep smoke going every night so the cattle could live. Thousands of cattle died, but we were fortunate and lost very few. The storm had filled the whole marsh near our house with lumber, debris and railroad ties from the railway which had washed away. Every evening we went to the marsh and hauled out a load of wood, built a fire and kept the smoke going to protect our cattle.

While the late summer of 1901 and the early summer of 1902 were almost intolerable because of the mosquitoes and the hardships with the stock, it was not without childhood memories of amusing incidents. Anthrax broke out among the cattle at Sabine Pass due to the mosquitoes and we lost a few. At that time we knew nothing of the necessity of burning the carcasses. It was a custom of my father to hitch a team of horses to the dead animal and drag it a long way from the house to the back of the pasture. One day my father came to the house and told my mother he would like to have an extra thick undershirt to prevent the mosquitoes from biting through his clothing. Jokingly he said in the presence of my younger sister, "I don't want the mos-

41

quitoes to eat me up and kill me." Lovie, who was three or four and apparently impressed by the scene of cattle being dragged off, said, "If they do kill you they ain't nobody got time to drag you off."

CHAPTER TEN

THE HORSE AND THE PROPER WAY TO BREAK HIM

A narrative of the events of the early days would be incomplete without some special reference to the horse. To the early Texan, the horse was a necessity for existence. Anyone who stole a horse was dealt with rather harshly. That fact may have given rise to the story of the New York lawyer who came to Texas and while talking with an old Texas Justice of the Peace asked, "Judge, why is it that you have such peculiar ideas of justice in Texas? Why, if a man kills another man and is tried, he'll probably come clear, but if a man steals a horse he'll be hanged." The old J.P. said to the lawyer, "There is nothing strange about that. We've got lots of people in Texas that need killing, but we sho ain't got no horses that need stealing."

We depended on the horse as our only means of transportation and power. Automobiles, trucks and tractors were unheard of. If we had to travel, we went on horseback or in a wagon, buggy or buckboard. A good cow pony would carry a man sixty or eighty miles in a day. Horses pulled our plows and other farming tools and, hitched to a wagon, took all of our products from place to place. I personally have hauled thousands of bushels of potatoes from our home at Hamshire to market in Beaumont, twenty miles away, in a two-horse wagon. This took from four a.m. until after dark that night. My father was the best horseman I ever knew. I do not mean that he was a famous rodeo broncbuster or a steer bulldogger. When he worked with horses and cattle, the work was done in a manner conducive to the raising and care of the animals. Any time Dad got hold of a horse, it would soon get fat and have a good saddle gait. We broke many wild horses in my younger days, or rather, we gentled them. The pictures you see on television and movies and the stories you read in western magazines about how horses are handled are fine for amusement, but far from the proper way to gentle and train horses for use on the farm and ranch. I never knew my father to abuse a horse in any manner or allow the horse to be unnecessarily hurt in the process of handling. He refused to rope a wild horse by the neck and let him choke himself down. I've seen him put a herd of wild stallions in a pen and, as they ran around the circle, he would decide which one he wanted and rope him expertly by the two front feet. When he was thrown in that manner, the only unpleasantness the horse suffered was in hitting the ground broadside with a thud. In addition, a ranchman and farmer in those days had to be a pretty good veterinarian. There was no doctor to call when your horse needed "doctoring".

Another important feature in the raising of horses was the castration of young stallions. Because of the nature of the development of a stallion, he cannot be castrated until he is two years of age and, if this operation is not done by an expert, the horse may bleed to death or die as a result of the operation. My father was an expert in this process. I can remember when I was a small child, ranchmen would bring herds of young stallions to my father's place. The cowboys would rope and throw them and Dad would perform the operation. On one occasion, when we were still living at Sabine Pass, Major McReynolds, who ran a lot of horses and cattle and raised a good many young horses, had his colored cowboys bring twenty-one stallions to my father's pen one Sunday morning. These cowboys did not rope the horses by the feet as Dad did, but roped them by the neck and choked them down. There were twenty-one young stallions in the pen. One big colored man made a big loop; he threw it and caught three stallions, together with a fence post in the loop. Old Major McReynolds, who never took an active part in the work, was sitting on the fence and yelled at the man to turn the rope loose. He did not do that. He pulled on the rope and the result was the three young stallions took down the whole side of the pen and all the horses escaped. I was a small child and I had never heard such profanity as came from the dignified old Major. They finally rebuilt the fence and penned the horses, working far into the late afternoon.

This operation was not cruel, but a necessity. It is safe to say that at breeding time the stallion is the most ferocious of the domestic animals. There is nothing more beautiful than a well-kept horse, no matter what the breed, and there is no scene that compares with the many activities of horses, including stallions in battle and in breeding. I hasten to say that this appeals not to the sensual, but to the esthetic. Stallions in battle will get in all kinds of positions; stand up on their hind feet and paw each other, bite each other, turn and kick each other as hard as possible with both hind feet, and continue until one is exhausted. They seem to have no more definite battle rules than men. A comparison between stallion fights and bull fights can be made. Thus, since the only means of transportation was the horse, the riding horses and the buggy horses, especially for the women, had to be either mares or geldings. To have used stallions as buggy horses would have been catastrophic. Even cowboys riding stallions to work cattle had to have a very severe quirt handy. An incident which occurred in the spring of 1974 should illustrate this vividly. I have handled all kinds of horses during my lifetime, from the sorriest little Southeast Texas prairie mustang to registered American saddle horses, which I used to breed and raise, but I have never known of an incident which reveals the danger as plainly.

Many times I have known a stallion, when crowded in a pen, to back his ears, bare his teeth, and make a threatening break toward a man. A whip would always turn him back. A stallion on the prairie with a bunch of mares will keep them in a close herd and, if one attempts to break away, will bring her back with threatening teeth and heels.

Recently a very fine cowboy, Tommy Webb, a second cousin of mine and the great-grandson of the W. J. Webb mentioned earlier, was working on a ranch. One of his duties was to look after a high-bred stallion and a herd of brood mares. Several times before the incident, he had ridden through the herd, cut out one or more of the mares and moved them to another pasture.

On the Sunday in question, he was not doing any work, but merely rode among the horses to look them over. He had ridden past the stallion, which was grazing with the mares, and had gone about fifty yards, sitting on his horse and looking over the herd. Suddenly, the stallion came tearing up behind him with his mouth wide open, grabbed him by the pocket of his Levis where his wallet was, taking Levis, wallet, flesh and all in the powerful grip of his teeth. After dragging him from his horse for about fifty yards, the Levis were torn completely off before he could free himself. He had to be taken to a doctor to have the bite treated and was on crutches for a week. Had it not been for the wallet, the wound would have been much worse.

Wild bulls on the prairie had an entirely different method of combat and most of their fighting was done in the spring of the year when competition was keen. During my teens, when I lived on the farm at Hamshire, there was absolutely no form of amusement and no social life of any kind. We worked so hard on weekdays in the fields and with the cattle we did not need any social life at night. However, we did not work in the fields on Sundays and, in the spring, my brother and I sometimes amused ourselves by bullfighting. The open prairie was full of cattle and a goodly number of bulls. Our fun

45

consisted of getting on our cow ponies, going to a herd on the range, picking out a bull we thought would put up a good fight, and drive him to another herd where there was another bull. By the time we got him there, he would be in a pretty bad humor. I don't think the bulls would have fought except that we promoted the fights by riding around them and yelling and popping our whips and the more noise we made the madder the bulls got. There was one little bull that belonged to Mr. Ben Hebert (we knew because it bore his brand) and we called him "Buffalo" because he had some of the appearance of a buffalo. For two or three years he was champion of the prairie. We would drive him from herd to herd on Sunday afternoons. He was always ready for a fight and always won.

It seemed that bulls had rules by which they fought. They would meet, face each other, paw the dust with their forefeet, bellow and finally work themselves up to the point where they were ready to fight. They would lunge at each other, head first, both pushing as hard as they could. Whether one could push the other depended a good deal upon the weight of the bull and the footing he had. They would push back and forth for awhile. Finally, if one, because of his weight and agility, would get a little advantage, he would push the other so fast that he could not run backwards anymore. The loser would turn and, as he turned, the winner would give him a hook in the ribs if he could reach his ribs. They never injured themselves much in fighting. The peculiar thing is that when one was finally out-pushed and made the turn, he never came back. He accepted that as a defeat and, as a rule, left the herd in a very bad mood.

Getting back to my father's method of gentling horses, I include a couple of instances as examples of the methods used. In my early teens, my father decided that my brother and I each needed a cow pony, so he made a trade with Mr. Arceneaux, a neighboring ranchman, to give him two steers for two ponies. That was a fair trade in those days because a three year old steer was worth about $15.00 and a cow pony about the same amount. He drove the steers to Mr. Arceneaux's ranch, about three miles away, on a day when he had a lot of young horses penned for breaking. He said we could have our pick of the herd. I picked a little sorrel pony, which I immediately named "Skewbald", and which made me a very faithful saddle and work horse for many years. I got the name from a little song I heard my uncle singing. I don't know where he got it, but it went something like this: "The horses were mounted and the word was given. Go! Old Skewbald, he started like an arrow from a bow."

My Dad roped the horse by the feet, threw him, and when the horse went down, a man got on his head and held his head down since a horse cannot get up unless he can raise his head. While the horse was down, a double rope was tied loosely around his neck and another tied in the loop. The rope ran from the loop down to one of the horse's hind feet, just above the hoof, and the other passed back through the loop on the neck. That rope pulled tighter until the horse had one hind leg hoisted very high when the horse was allowed to get up. He could not run; he could not buck; he could not rear up; he couldn't do anything but stand there. A hackamore was placed on him; we didn't put a bridle on the horse when he was first ridden. Hackamore is a halter which is made of very strong rope and fits around the horse's head, nose and under his throat. A long rope was tied to the hackamore under the horse's throat and the horse saddled while he stood.

On this occasion, Dad was riding a big strong horse. He fastened the rope, which was tied to the hackamore, to his saddle pommel, giving the horse about two feet. There was nothing the horse could do; he could not rear up and could not get his head down to buck. I got on the horse and rode it home in that manner. The horse was never allowed to buck and, in fact, I guess he never learned he could buck. After a few such ridings, the horse was ready to be handled alone.

Many years later, after Dad was seventy years of age and I was traveling, I came home one Sunday and he told me he wanted me to help him catch a wild horse he had bought. He had bought from Mr. Gill a little black stallion which was running with wild horses on the range. He had several boys helping him the Sunday before. They had run the horses down but were unable to pen the herd. Together with some neighbors, I went with him. After much running, we finally penned the herd at Joe Craigen's place, about seven miles from our home. This was one of the prettiest little horses I have ever seen. We caught him and saddled him in the same manner as years before and I rode the horse home tied to my father's pommel. The next week I came out and gave him a ride in the same manner. Two weeks later I came home one Sunday and Dad was riding the horse down the road alone. This little horse was so fast and such a good roping horse that Dad finally sold him to a rodeo man.

My personal experiences with horses have been many. Since I first acquired the little sorrel pony, Skewbald, I owned many work and saddle horses. They ranged all the way from very small scrub prairie cow ponies to American saddle horses, which I raised on the farm, and which became valuable show horses. In later years, they won many ribbons. That kind of horse raising is not what I am emphasizing; I am stressing the importance of the horse to man's existence in the early days.

Sometimes the horse meant the difference between life and death. I think it was about the year 1904 when my brother and my oldest sister became very sick with typhoid fever. There was no doctor in this area and no drugstores closer than Beaumont. My father managed to get to a telephone and call a doctor who came out in an automobile, which was only the second automobile I had ever seen. I was working around the barn while the doctor was there. My father came out and very quietly saddled his favorite horse, Old Dan, a horse that we boys were seldom allowed to ride. He called me and told me to get on Old Dan and ride to Beaumont, twenty miles away. I was told to hitch my horse at the water trough at the courthouse. I knew how to get to the courthouse because I had been there the previous year in a two-horse wagon with my uncle. He said, "Let your horse drink, but not too much, and give him thirty minutes to rest while you walk to Grimes and Hurst Drugstore four blocks up the street. Some medicine will be waiting for you." Dad said, "Get the medicine, and come back after your horse has rested. Do not ride too fast; let Old Dan choose his gait." When Old Dan chose his gait, it was the most comfortable saddle gait that anyone ever experienced. It was just like an easy rocking chair. I was delighted to get to ride Dan, but of course was worried about the condition of my brother and sister. I got back at two a.m. I was very tired and ready for bed. Dad met me, took the medicine, and unsaddled Dan. The next morning he reported my brother and sister were better.

CHAPTER ELEVEN

THE FIDDLE AND THE ODORIFEROUS ORGAN

Readers of this work may get the impression from what has been said in former chapters that all of our pioneer life was hard work and monotonous, but this is not true. Life had a brighter side from the children's standpoint. Our parents were very religious and good people. There was a period of time from about 1902 until 1913 when there was no church that we could reach in a two-horse wagon. From the time I can first remember, my mother had an old-fashioned organ which stood in the corner of the living room of the old homestead. I do not know the source of this organ or during what period of time our mother acquired it. In her early girlhood she lived with her parents on a cotton plantation in Mississippi. Since they were at that time in good circumstances, she was given music lessons. She not only had a good voice for singing, but she was expert in getting music out of that old organ.

My father was what we used to call an old-time fiddler. I have never known anyone who could get more melody out of a violin. He could not read a note of music, but played from ear. The combination of the organ and violin made the best music I have ever heard.

I am not at all partial to piano music. If I wanted to make a comparison between the music they made and that produced by the famous Liberace (and I attended his piano recital in New York City) I would say the music my parents made was comparable to the music produced by the Mormon Temple in Salt Lake City and the so-called music by Liberace was no more musical than the sound produced by water dripping from a roof on a rainy night on to the bottom of an old tin wash tub.

Regardless of my prejudice and why it existed, I must continue. Every Sunday night, during the period when we had no church, my mother would take her place at the organ with Dad close by in a chair with his violin. All the children and any visitors who might be present would gather around and sing old-time spiritual songs. I may not agree one hundred percent with the theology expressed in the songs, but it was fine music and very good for the spiritual and moral welfare of us teenage children.

I will never forget the words and music of many of them. For instance:

Life's Railway to Heaven
Life is like a mountain railroad,
With an engineer that's brave
You must make the run successful
From the cradle to the grave.

Watch for curves and mind the trestles
They will almost wreck your train
Always mindful of obstructions
Watch for storms of wind and hail
Keep your hand upon the throttle
And your eye upon the rail.

Another:

The Rock of Ages
Rock of ages cleft for me,
Let me hide myself in thee
Let the water and the blood
From thy wounded side which flowed
Be of sin, a double cure
Save from wrath and make me pure.

Another:

Beautiful River
Shall we gather at the river
Where bright angel feet have trod
With its crystal light forever
Flowing by the throne of God.

We did not have locks on the doors of our house and, at this time, there was not even a latch on the back screen door. If a traveler came through when we were away from home and got some food for his immediate needs, we were happy about it. From the year 1895 to 1916, when the old house was abandoned, not one item was ever stolen. The following story resulted from this unlatched screen door and succeeded in interrupting our Sunday night services.

We had a lot of chickens on the farm and they produced a lot of eggs. It was the job of my younger sister, who was about thirteen years of age, to gather the eggs from the hen house every evening. She placed them in a large water bucket just inside the kitchen back door. My mother would take the eggs she needed for the family and would let my sister take the rest to the local grocery store and sell them for ten cents per dozen. She was allowed to have the proceeds as spending money.

One night my mother made the remark that rats were getting into the eggs which she knew because of having seen empty shells near the bucket. My sister, wanting to protect her source of income, asked me to go to the barn and get one of my steel traps which I used for trapping "coons." I did as she requested, and set the trap by opening the jaws and placing the trigger in the proper position. My sister laid the trap by the bucket of eggs and did not bait it, nor did she make the chain fast to anything, believing the heavy steel trap would kill the rat if it stepped on the trigger.

We all went to bed as usual. My father was awakened by a terrible noise as if something was being dragged through the house. Immediately upon awaking, he smelled a familiar odor. The first thing we children knew about the matter was when Dad hollered to us saying not to get out of bed until he could light the lamp because there was a skunk in the house. My sister who had set the trap was also awakened and heard what my father said. Not being as familiar with the odor as the others, she laughingly said, "Papa thinks that's a polecat, but it's not. I set that trap for a rat," and went back to sleep.

Dad finally got the kerosene lamp lit and from the noise and smell managed to trace the skunk dragging the trap through three rooms, to where he had hidden himself, trap and all, in my mother's organ in the living room.

By that time the odor had gotten so intense there was nothing to do but get the organ out of the house. So Dad, with the help of us two boys, carried it out (trap, skunk and all) and set it on the front porch. Dad retrieved the trap and skunk from the organ the next day, but he could not "retrieve" the scent. What the organ emitted the next two months was anything but sweet music. It was two months before our mother would allow the organ brought back into the living room. Even then, she was not entirely happy with the odor to which she remained very sensitive.

Every animal has its own defense system: a possum will lie down and play dead on the first contact with the enemy, a raccoon will fight with his teeth and claws, a rabbit has his fast speed, but the skunk has nothing but the odor which is a terrible musk and which can be discharged when attacked. With the large black skunk this is so intense that it cannot be tolerated on close contact. I have seen my hunting dog, not knowing the danger, attack a skunk and be entirely "knocked out" like a person being chloroformed. I used to hunt them for their skins. I was very careful and would shoot them on sight before their musk could be discharged; but, in spite of that precaution, when I came back from a polecat hunt my mother would make me go to the barn, change my clothes and take a bath before she would let me come into the house.

CHAPTER TWELVE

FROM DISASTER TO WEALTH

I do not believe the story of Hamshire, Texas would be complete, without special reference to Lovan Hamshire, the very fine gentleman for whom the town was named. The following story may not be absolutely accurate, but this is the way it was told to me and I know it is substantially true. As it certainly does not discredit anyone, I will relate it with apologies for any inaccuracies.

I worked for Mr. Hamshire when I was about 14 years old, before we bought his cane mill, as related earlier. The old Hamshire home still stands about two miles east of Hamshire and is maintained for family reunions by Eunice Hamshire Arceneaux, one of the several very fine daughters that he and his wife reared.

About 1864, Eloi Broussard died and left his widow who was the daughter of Joe Hebert, the father of several Hebert men who were ranchmen and lived near Beaumont. There was born to Eloi Broussard and his wife, Esma, one child, a boy by the name of Joe, who was about 10 years old at the time of his father's death. His mother did not remain a widow long, and married Lovan Hamshire who became Joe's legal guardian. The Probate Code was much the same then as now. One half of the community estate of Eloi Broussard and his wife legally belonged to the only son, Joe. This half had been converted to cash and amounted to $10,000. Mr. Hamshire was holding this money, waiting for an opportunity to invest it in cattle, the only wise investment at the time. Since most of the land belonged to the State and the ranchmen ran their cattle on entirely rent-free land, cattlemen considered an investment in land foolish.

The nearest bank was in New Orleans. The only iron safe in Beaumont belonged to a man who ran a general store, selling everything the ranchmen and lumbermen needed from pins to log wagons. I do not recall the merchant's name, but he was trusted by the ranchmen and many of them left their cash with him for safe keeping in his safe. Lovan Hamshire left Joe's $10,000 there.

This merchant had some foresight as to the probable increase in land values. There were thousands of acres of good black land in the China area, about 15 miles west of Beaumont, which could be bought for 25¢ an acre from the state. He formed the habit of driving out there in his buckboard on Sundays, picking out the best sections of land and buying it. The ranchmen thought him foolish, since trail drivers had started to Kansas and a good steer would bring $15. Thus, the old fellow owned a lot of land which he bought, no doubt, with his own money.

However, about that time, in order to further his search after wealth, he started a less safe venture. He started gambling in the stock market. I know nothing about gambling in futures, but I understand if the commodity you have bought starts going down you have to put up more money to protect your investment. It seems the old fellow had guessed wrong and bought too heavily in a commodity that went down and he had to put up a lot of money to protect his investment. When his own cash was exhausted, he began to use his friends' money in large quantities, including Joe's $10,000.

When the news broke out as to what had happened, some of Joe's uncles, the Heberts who lived in Beaumont, heard of it first and sent word to Lovan Hamshire, who was then at a cattle round up at Little Pine Island, approximately 30 miles southwest of Beaumont. Bear in mind this event was about 100 years ago. There were no telephones and no automobiles. The Heberts in Beaumont sent word to Lovan by horseback messenger and, in doing so, provided for a relay of three cow ponies. As a result, Lovan was the first to reach the old fellow (fortunately for Joe, and I believe for the country as a whole).

I do not know just what happened when Lovan reached the merchant's store, but I will say that when I worked for Lovan many years later, he was still a tall raw-boned man and weighed over 200 pounds. At any rate, after a conference in the back room of the store, they both emerged, looked up a notary public and a deed was drawn up giving Joe all of the land the old merchant owned in Jefferson County for the consideration of $10,000.

Lovan rode back to the ranch, called his wife and stepson in and told them the sad story. The $10,000 was lost and all the 10 year old boy, Joe, had to show for it was the old "no-account land." As related earlier, about the turn

54

of the century, rice farming, which depended upon timely rains, had failed. Joe's large land holdings were not far from Pine Island Bayou, a branch of the Neches River, where there was an abundance of fresh water. East Texas is in the 54-inch rain belt and the Neches River had always had and always will have an adequate supply of water.

When Joe reached manhood, he saw the opportunity to build a canal from Pine Island Bayou through his "no account land." This canal operated for many years as the Beaumont Irrigation Company. Joe also built the Beaumont Rice Mill which is still being operated. That "unfortunate incident," the loss of the $10,000, was the beginning of the rice industry which has contributed, and still contributes many millions to the economy of the country and the welfare of the people.

Joe, a very rich man, was also a very good man. He did a lot of good with his money and helped a lot of poor farmers get a start to prosperity. I had many dealings with him in later years, respected him as a good and fair man and considered him a great philanthropist. Of course, all rich men make enemies and some people dislike them, but I say he was a good man. Turning misfortune into fortune seemed to be his life pattern. Mr. Herbert Roedenbeck, another good man who will be mentioned later in this work, was in real estate in this area for over half a century. He told me that in his time he had sold Joe six oil fields, land which was thought of as of little value, which later became oil-producing land.

The following narrative may be interesting in this connection. About the year 1935, as a lawyer, I was employed by some Houston lawyers to assist in a trial pending in Chambers County. The lawsuit was styled "Roedenbeck Farms, Inc. vs J. E. Broussard." This case involved 21 lawyers, took 21 days of trial in the District Court at Anahuac and went to the Supreme Court of the United States.

Roedenbeck and some associates, under the name of Roedenbeck Farms, Inc., had acquired considerable land in the vicinity of where the Anahuac Oil Field is located. They were farming rice on a rather large scale. Needing money for operations, the corporation borrowed $5.00 per acre on this particular section and, as a result of the dramatic price reductions that followed World War I, they went broke as most farmers did. Broussard, who had money to lend on rice farms, was merely trying to secure a reasonable interest on his money. The loan was secured by a deed of trust on this section. In Texas a deed of trust is a form of mortgage to secure notes on which land is given as security. The deed of trust gives the holder of the note the right to call upon the trustee named in the deed of trust to sell the land to satisfy the note if the maker of the note defaults in payment. The depression was underway and Roedenbeck Farms, Inc. could not meet the note.

The note lacked only a few days of becoming void by the limitation statutes when Broussard called upon the trustee to sell the land. Broussard did not want the land, values of which were nearly zero at the time. After the mortgage was made, Roedenbeck Farms, Inc. sold the section to three different people. Of course, these sales did not affect Broussard's liens, but, because of peculiar wording in the deed of trust, the legal question involved was whether Broussard's trustee should have given the purchasers from Roedenbeck notice of the trustee's sale. However, at the sale, Broussard bid the land in for the amount of the note with interest, which probably at that time was less than $10.00 per acre. No one else wanted the land at that price.

Soon after, an independent oil man, a redheaded Irishman by the name of Glenn McCarthy, drilled a wild-cat well in the area which developed into the very large and rich Anahuac Oil Field. When this well came in, the major companies made a rush for leases and the Humble Company, about two years after he bought the land, leased it from Broussard for as much as it cost him. Two years later we were trying the law suit. By this time the section had twelve producing wells on it and the attorneys for the Humble Company told me that Broussard's royalty interest was worth $3,000,000.

The Humble Company made the lease and, being anxious to drill, had examined the title and, seeing a possible flaw by reason of the failure of the trustee to give the purchasers notice of the sale, they gave these purchasers $75,000 to ratify the lease so they could safely produce oil.

In the controversy between Broussard and the purchasers over the royalty interest, Broussard won; but, in the paying of the $75,000, Humble had financed a nice big lawsuit.

CHAPTER THIRTEEN

THE DISCOVERY OF OIL IN BEAUMONT

No event had a greater effect upon the economy of Southeast Texas and the lives and welfare of the area than the discovery of oil at Spindletop near Beaumont in 1901. Having been nine years old at the time and, having a fair memory of happenings over three quarters of a century, I am in a position to give a summary account of those events.

Prior to 1900 there was, of course, petroleum produced in parts of the United States. There were oil fields in Pennsylvania, but the fields were spread over a large area, and the wells were small producers, creating little excitement. There was also a producing field at Corsicana, Texas, but when Lucas drilled a well at Spindletop, about five miles south of Beaumont, he struck a tremendous gusher at 1,050 feet. The production was phenomenal. The well went wild and produced thousands of barrels of oil per day. Beaumont became a boom town. Many came there to organize oil companies, lease land and drill wells. It was believed by some that this heavy production would extend over the entire county. But it finally developed that this shallow production covered an area of not more than 250 acres. In some places the wells were drilled so close together that a person could step from one derrick platform to another. However, many wells were drilled throughout the entire county and were dry holes. We were living at Sabine Pass at the time and, when we moved back to our home at Hamshire, twenty miles from Spindletop, there were five derricks in sight, all dry holes.

To illustrate this situation, I will tell the following experience I had many years later. I was in Boston in 1925 as a salesman of figs which we were packing in our Hamshire Fig Preserving Plant. I was introduced to a fine old gentleman who was the owner of a wholesale grocery house in Boston. When he was told that I was from Beaumont, he wheeled his office chair back from his desk, looked up at me and said: "Beaumont brings back sad memories." I said, "Why sad memories?" He said, "Do you remember the oil boom in 1901?" I said, "Yes, I do." He said, "The story of the Lucas gusher created so much excitement here in Boston that nine other businessmen here in town and I put up $10,000 each, organized a company and took a lease on a piece of land about twenty miles from Beaumont. It looked close to the Lucas Gusher on the map that was shown us. Of course, we lost the whole $100,000." However, I sold him a nice order of figs packed by the Beaumont-Hamshire Fig Company. These figs were grown on about 1,200 acres of orchards we had in the Hamshire area at that time.

There is another side of the coin. The jokes, stories, and television stories about Texas oil millionaires are not entirely without foundation. I can give you the following illustration from my own personal knowledge. If this history is not entirely correct, I apologize for any discrepancies, but there is certainly nothing in my memory that would detract from the high character of the men involved. When we returned to Hamshire in 1902, C. T. Heisig was a real estate man in Beaumont. We later became very close friends. We had in common the fact that we were both raised on a farm and had gone into other businesses. It seems that a farm boy cannot ever get it out of his blood and when he starts to playing with the things he worked with as a boy, he usually finds it is an excellent way to lose money.

By 1902, Heisig had acquired three sections of land about two miles from my home and was raising rice. He had employed a young man by the name of Frank Yount as farm manager and was paying him $60.00 per month. (As a boy, I worked for Frank on that farm for $1.00 per day.)

Mr. Heisig, having such a large farming operation, bought a big J. I. Case thrashing machine powered by a steam engine. Frank was such a capable and industrious man that he could get his rice thrashed early and take the crew to neighboring farms to thrash their rice. The farmers liked to have Frank come to their fields because he got the work done quickly and efficiently. Many years later, after Frank had become a multimillion dollar oil man, Mr. Heisig and I had occasion to visit him at his office in Beaumont on a matter of business. He proudly showed us a medal that the J. I. Case thrashing machine company had given him because he had thrashed more rice in a day with their machine than any other man. This quality in Frank was, I think, responsible for his phenomenal success in the oil business.

Frank left the farm and the $60.00 a month job and went to work in the Spindletop Oil Field. He soon became a driller, then acquired a rig of his own. And, believing that oil could be found deeper, he acquired leases on the fringe of the old field. Due to his industry and his fair dealings with everyone (including his employees), at the time of his untimely death in his fifties he was many times a millionaire. He had been using his money not only in the oil business, but in the development of his home town of Beaumont. It is my belief that had he lived, Beaumont would have been a more prosperous city today.

Similar history could be given of several men I knew personally. Of course, many fortunes were lost and many made, but, as better exploration and drilling methods were found and oil production spread to all of Southeast Texas, you could not travel even a short distance in this area without observing oil production. The result was that the strictly farming and ranching community was changed to a highly industrial and oil-producing territory. It has often been said that there is nothing more beneficial to a farmer or rancher in financial distress than a few oil wells scattered around on his place.

Deep water was brought to Port Arthur at a very opportune time. When oil was discovered, it was an ideal place for the construction of large refineries. It grew from a village of three houses when I passed through there in 1897 to its present status as a fine city.

For some reason, Beaumont never did enjoy the natural benefits which should have resulted from the discovery at Spindletop. Gas and oil discoveries spread over the entire area and Houston became the oil center of the south. In a few years it became a city of over a million inhabitants, the headquarters of many oil companies and oil operators and the financial center of the entire industry.

Another interesting point is that, about the time oil was discovered in vast quantities, the internal combustion engine was invented with the result that petroleum and petroleum products had a great effect on the economy of the entire world. In 1901, when oil was discovered in Beaumont, petroleum was selling for ten cents a barrel and, now in 1976, its products are in world-wide use and we are hearing rumors of a potential energy crisis.

CHAPTER FOURTEEN

THE ORANGE BOOM

In recording events of the area during the past three quarters of the century, it may be well to refer to what I call the Orange Boom. In an earlier chapter, there is a record of a Providence rice boom, which caused many settlers to migrate to this part of the country. Among the very few who remained was a man by the name of Spencer, who planted ten acres of Satsuma oranges near the little town of Stowell, Texas. There were several mild winters with no freezes. The orchard was beautiful. From the standpoint of beauty, nothing in California or Florida can compare with the Texas Satsuma orange orchard in full production, if it has escaped freezing weather for six winters. And there is nothing more deceptive from the standpoint of a safe investment.

Two real estate men from the North, Theodore F. Koch, with whom I worked many years later in the real estate and fig packing business, and M. E. Wilson, learning of and seeing this magnificent orange orchard, conceived the idea of buying a vast amount of land in the Winnie-Hamshire area. They brought in many settlers from the north, sold them land during the years of 1912 and 1913 and many small orchards were planted. This seemed very attractive for, because of the heavy rainfall in this area, irrigation would not be required as in California and the Rio Grande Valley. The largest orchard of which I had knowledge was seventy acres planted by Koch himself, which adjoined my place and was right across the road from my present pecan grove. This orchard enjoyed about four years of mild winters and was simply beautiful. Koch, realizing that a freeze might come and knowing the method of heating orchards by smudge pots, arranged for thus protecting his orchard from freeze. He bought a carload of petroleum and hundreds of smudge pots. We did not have radio and television warning of approaching freezes in those days but the weather indicated that a freeze was coming. Koch's foremen and a large crew filled the smudge pots the evening before the freeze. He set his alarm clock so he could wake up at two a.m. and light his smudge pots. The alarm clock did not go off. The orchard froze, along with the other small orchards in the community, and that was the end of the orange boom in the Hamshire-Winnie area.

CHAPTER FIFTEEN

THE FIG BOOM

Some time prior to 1915, a very energetic and competent man by the name of Carpenter, who was an accountant, came to Houston from Kansas and married a Houston girl whose mother had a backyard fig orchard in the northern part of the city. I do not know of anyone who knows the origin of the variety called Magnolia fig, but they were outstanding from the standpoint of production and the quality of preserves they made. Carpenter was so impressed with this fruit that he conceived the idea of growing and packing these figs commercially. He procured cuttings, planted an orchard and built a small preserving plant at Friendswood, south of Houston. He also encouraged neighboring farmers to plant small orchards to supply his plant and the J. C. Carpenter Company prospered for several years.

He learned that several very thrifty German farmers had survived the catastrophe of the orange business in the Hamshire-Winnie area, persuaded several of them to plant small fig orchards and built a small preserving plant at Winnie.

His market was limited to supplying figs to the dining car services and other services where price was not a major consideration. He told me he conceived the idea of packing a small five-ounce jar and selling his figs to the railroad for dining car service, believing that those persons traveling on trains would get a taste of Texas figs and, therefore, would create a universal market. His theory was bad. Although travel by train was important in those days, he failed to consider that a very small percentage of what we called the "ham-and-egg public" ever traveled in dining cars. Furthermore, because of the expense of gathering and processing, Magnolia figs could not compete in price with other soft fruits. It made little difference that the packing plant paid only five cents a pound for the figs that went into the five-ounce containers that sold for thirty-five cents each. As a specialty, it was a fine business, but as a staple it was a failure and the market, as a specialty, was very limited. For example, on the Thursday before Good Friday, in 1925, I was in Montreal, Canada, as a salesman. I sold the buyer for the dining car service of Canadian National Railroad a car load of these five-ounce jars. He said when he signed the contract, "Now that is all the figs I will need for two years, so you do not need to come back." Now the Canadian National Railroad traversed the continent and had hundreds of dining cars.

In 1925, when rice was selling for three dollars a barrel and cotton at ten cents a pound, a fig orchard, with figs selling at five cents a pound, would produce $500 per acre. So, there was a wild rush to plant figs and build preserving plants in Southeast Texas. The Koch Land Company mentioned above, had started its operations here in 1912, and had brought in many settlers as a result of the orange boom. The company was entirely owned by Germans, still in Germany, except for the interest of Mr. Koch. When World War I broke out between the United States and Germany, these properties were taken over by the alien custodians and all operations ceased.

In the meantime, the Germans who had survived the orange catastrophe had planted the small fig orchards to supply the Carpenter Fig Factory at Winnie, Texas. In 1921 Mr. Koch saw, or thought he saw, a great opportunity and bought out his German associates. These beautiful fig orchards were yielding $500 per acre. He conceived the idea of reopening his land business and selling land on the strength of figs instead of oranges, another incident where beautiful orchards caused a catastrophe.

I went to work for Koch as a land salesman in 1921. Neither he, a real estate promoter, nor I, a farm boy, had sense enough to know that we could not make a staple food product out of a fruit which was so expensive to produce and process. It could not meet competition as a staple article of fruit and its demand was limited to a specialty market. By 1924, our land customers had 1,200 acres of beautiful orchards in the Hamshire area. The little plant at Winnie could not begin to take care of production so we organized a corporation and built a plant at Hamshire in which I invested my life savings of $5,000. The company was called The Beaumont-Hamshire Fig Company, of which I was general manager. While we were doing this, fifteen other plants were built in Southeast Texas to take care of similar fig farms in their area and by 1926, there were thousands of acres and seventeen preserving plants. Production had increased from 45,000 cases in 1921 to 385,000 cases in 1926. Everybody connected with it went broke, including myself.

The Magnolia fig was a peculiar plant. Growth was so rapid in this coast country, that an orchard two years of age would produce a paying crop and, at five years of age, would reach its maximum capacity. The trees were pruned severely each year, resulting in new limb growth of six to eight feet and, because figs bear on the current year's growth, one at each leaf, the harvest hand would begin picking in July and finish the top of the limb in November. It can readily be seen that the harvest hand would have to visit the trees every day for perhaps 100 days, getting only a few figs each day. As a result, even with cheap labor, it cost more to simply harvest Magnolia figs than it did to produce, harvest and deliver the other competitive soft fruits.

Another costly item was the peeling. The fruit was so tender it could not be peeled by machinery. In our small plant, we would have as many as one hundred girls peeling figs and preparing them for the cooking kettles. Another expense was the vast amount of sugar required to make a tasty preserve. When the family sized jar of preserved Magnolia figs reached the grocery shelf, it could not be sold for less than thirty-five cents, while its competitors, such as apple butter and peach preserves, could sell for twenty or twenty-five cents. We could never educate the buying public to cultivate a taste for Magnolia figs, unpeeled and unpreserved. The following narrative may illustrate this point. Southern Europeans and their descendants residing in the heavily populated area in the New England states were accustomed to eating dried figs. They were shipped in by boat from Smyrna to New York and served like stewed prunes in the cheap cafes. However, they were much tougher than prunes and, so far as this writer is concerned, their texture could be compared to rawhide. Nevertheless, that product was what the trade wanted.

In our struggle to meet competition in prices, our plant manager conceived the idea of putting up figs in large cans. They were unpeeled, unpreserved and in a light syrup. He packed several car loads in large cans, which could have sold in competition with canned peaches. We Southerners thought they were fine served with cream and sugar, but there was one problem: they did not sell.

Representing our factory, I was in New York, working with our broker. At that time the four largest buyers of canned goods were the A & P Company, Seaman Bros., Francis J. Liggett and Austin Nichols, "the big four." We were having hard sledding in greater New York in our attempt to put our product on the market. One day the broker said to me, "McCall, I believe that Austin Nichols' buyer in Jersey City has an outlet that could handle your fresh figs. We enthusiastically took the bus and went to Jersey City. The broker introduced me to the buyer, a hardboiled New Yorker, whose work required him to taste canned goods all day. I handed the buyer a can of our so-called fresh figs and, while he was opening the can, gave him a long spiel about how we had spent time and effort in the perfection of an article which would taste like a fresh fig, right off the tree, and I believed that we had succeeded. By the time I had finished my discourse, he had taken a large fig in his mouth, spit it out, and said, "Yes, it tastes like a fresh fig, but who in hell wants a fresh fig?" Needless to say, I did not make the sale.

Because I was so completely identified with the production and marketing of figs, I perhaps was the first to see the handwriting on the wall. I converted my fig orchard into a pecan orchard. In 1927, I planted a paper shell pecan tree between every third fig tree on every third row of my fig orchard, and when the fig business was completely dead, I removed the fig trees.

I do not say that birth place and its environments affect a man's later life. However, found among the possessions of my sister, there is a picture of my brother, my sister and I at the old Johnson place where I was born. There were about twenty large pecan trees on that place. When the picture was taken, I was two years of age and my father was a tenant farmer on this farm. Now I have on my farm at Hamshire a twenty-acre pecan grove which I believe is one of the most beautiful scenes in the county. This grove, to me, is a hobby from which I make a profit some years. In 1975, I harvested and sold 20,000 pounds of paper-shell pecans. I have a small building nearby where these pecans are stored, shelled, and sold. Some of my friends jokingly refer to this building as McCall's Nut House. But I tell them that unlike most of their expensive hobbies, mine is making a profit.

CHAPTER SIXTEEN

●

THE FORTY-FIVE SO BIG IT SAVED MY LIFE

Prior to beginning the practice of law, I was a deputy sheriff. I do not believe I made a very great success as a peace officer. However, there is one incident that occurred during that time which may add something to this narrative.

In 1913, the year I was 21, the farmers and ranchers of the area voted on and approved a stock law. Because the law contained a provision that it must be enforced by a sheriff or constable and, since there was no constable, they had to have the county sheriff appoint a deputy. I suppose they concluded that since I was not much good for anything else, I would make a good deputy. So they petitioned the county sheriff to appoint me deputy sheriff. When the petition was circulated a very good friend and neighbor of mine said, "Yes, I'll sign the petition. Since we don't need a deputy sheriff, I think you would be a good man for the job." I was appointed deputy sheriff and, of course, being very proud of the appointment, I immediately acquired a badge and a big forty-five six-shooter. What young man of that day and time would not be proud of the right to carry a six-shooter? I did not know it then but, because of the large size of the forty-five, it saved my life.

I had made several arrests and it was unusual that any person, especially a black person, would resist arrest. For example, just prior to the incident in question, I had received a warrant from a sheriff in Louisiana, requesting the arrest of a certain black man. The Louisiana sheriff told me that this man was accused of stealing a gray horse from a farmer in Louisiana and was reported to be working on a big rice farm about three miles from my home. I saddled my horse, buckled on my six-shooter and rode to the farm. The foreman was on his horse overseeing about a dozen men shocking rice in the field. I rode up to the foreman and asked, "Do you have a man working for you by the name of _____?" He said, "Yes, he's right over there by that rice shock." I rode over and I said to him, calling his name, "I have a warrant for your arrest; you are wanted in Louisiana for stealing a horse."

"Sir?"

"You are wanted in Louisiana for stealing a horse."

"That white man knows I didn't steal that horse, I just borrowed that horse to ride to town and I turned him loose and I know he went home."

I said, "Well, I have a warrant and I have to take you in." Without any resistance whatsoever, he accompanied me, we caught the train to Beaumont and I turned him over to the sheriff of Jefferson County, so the sheriff in Louisiana could come for him. On the way in, he told me that he had not stolen the horse, that he was working on a farm in Louisiana and had told his boss that he had an offer of a job in Texas. He wanted to borrow a horse to ride to town to catch a train and would turn the horse loose, knowing the horse would go home. I guess the situation was as he told it and perhaps the old horse strayed away and didn't go home and the farmer thought he had stolen the horse. However, I told him to tell it to the judge just as he did to me and I thought he would get out of it all right. The result was that he was back on the farm in about three days.

Shortly after, I arrested a man for carrying a gun. He very willingly handed it over to me with no resistance. As a result, I was not accustomed to having persons whom I sought resist arrest. At the time of the incident, I had gone to Sunday school dressed in a palm beach suit and straw hat, thinking I looked very nice. Before Sunday school started, a local boy came to the church house and told me that the Negroes were having some trouble at the local post office and I was needed. I walked on to my home about a quarter of a mile away and, while passing the post office, I was approached by a big black man who was called "Frenchie." I knew him very well because he was what was called "corral boss" of a large rice farm and traded frequently in my father's grocery store. About an eighth of a mile from the grocery store where I stopped was a depot. Frenchie said, "Mr. LeRoy, look down there. You see that woman sitting on that stool ready to get on that train when it comes by?"

"Yes."

"You see that man standing out there about fifty feet from her behind that telegraph pole?"

"Yes."

"Well, that's my woman. I brought her from Louisiana and she was cooking on my boss's farm and I was corral boss."

Now the job of the corral boss was to take care of all of the mules and feed them, to "rustle" groceries and keep things up around the place while the rest of the hands were working around the field. He said, "She and I were saving all the money both of us made and we were going to save a good stake and go back to Louisiana. And this man you see standing out there, he just got out of the penitentiary and he claimed this was his woman before he left. He went to the farm yesterday while I was gone, took this woman and all our money and now he is going to take her and the money back to Louisiana."

I said, "Well Frenchie, that's a civil matter. I cannot arrest this man because he has taken a woman you claim and money you claim, but if he is carrying a gun I have a right to arrest him because that's a violation of the laws of the State of Texas."

"Well, he's carrying a gun all right! And he's dangerous. And he's carrying that gun where he can reach it with his right hand or his left hand and, white folks, he's dangerous."

I said, "Well, I'm not concerned over that. I don't believe he will give me any trouble. I'll go to my home, get my gun and come back and arrest him."

I went to my home, took my forty-five out of the drawer and started to buckle it on. It then occurred to me that if I went to Beaumont on that train after arresting this man, I would have about six hours to wait before the train would come back in the afternoon. There was a certain girl in Beaumont I very much desired to visit. I couldn't see myself calling on this girl with this forty-five buckled on my white palm beach suit. I said to myself, "Well, there will be no trouble, I'll just put the gun back in the drawer." I walked on down without the gun. I passed by where Frenchie was with several white and black men and on to the depot. The whole gang followed me to see the fun.

When I got there, this fellow was standing about fifty feet away from the depot near a telegraph pole and the woman was sitting on a box near where the train would stop. The train was only a few minutes down the track coming from Galveston to Beaumont. When I walked up, with these men and boys following me, I said, "I want to talk to you." He said, "No Sir, I'm not coming over there. That gang you've got would gang up on me and I wouldn't have a chance." I turned around and said, "Boys, go in the depot and leave us alone; I want to talk to this man."

After they left, he started cussing the black man, Frenchie. He told me that he was a white man; although, judging by his color, the statement was only partially true. He said, "I'm a white man and he's a nigger. I was in the penitentiary and, while in the penitentiary, he stole my woman. Now if this was in Louisiana they wouldn't let a nigger do a white man that way."

He was very vindictive and very angry because his woman had been stolen by a "nigger." I said, "Well, I have nothing to do with your controversy over the woman, that's between you and Frenchie, but you are carrying a gun in violation of the laws of the State of Texas. And I want you to hand me that gun now or I'll take you to jail."

He said, "No Sir. I've been arrested five times, the last time I was arrested I served five years in the penitentiary and I ain't gonna be arrested no more." He stepped over behind the telegraph pole and shoved his coat back to where his gun was in plain view. I don't know whether he knew at the time that I was unarmed; nevertheless, he was ready for any emergency.

This of course made me very unhappy. My unhappiness was mingled with some anger. With a sizeable audience looking on, here was a Texas deputy successfully resisted by a Louisiana black man. However, I shudder to think what would have happened if I had had my gun on. I've often been very thankful that I intended to go see the girl and didn't want to carry that big forty-five.

I went back into the depot and asked the boys if anyone had an automobile that could take me to town to meet that train. There was no automobile available but one neighbor boy had a motorcycle. He said, "I can get you to town before that train gets there."

I said, "All right, I'll ride the motorcycle with you, I'll call the court house, have the sheriff to meet me at the train and we'll arrest that man." That was arranged. About that time, as the train approached, the man from Louisiana said something in French to the woman and she moved over near the platform where the passengers would get on the train. He moved about 100 yards down the track toward Beaumont and toward a woods about a half a mile away. I fully expected him to board the train as it passed him. Frenchie, apparently not afraid of him, approached him and they were talking in French.

Among other things the Louisiana man said to Frenchie, after cursing him severely, was, "If you come another step toward me, I'll kill you."

Frenchie turned back. The train pulled up and the woman and Frenchie got on the train. The train pulled out and, instead of boarding the train, this fellow lit out toward the woods, in a full run, and that was the last I ever saw of him. I thought, "Well, Frenchie got his woman back, he got his money back and this man is not on the train, so all the State of Texas has against him is carrying a gun, so I'm not going to pursue it any further."

A few days later, I met Mr. Nolte, the foreman of the farm where Frenchie and the woman worked. He knew of my run-in with this man. He said to me, "LeRoy, you remember that fellow you had the run-in with?"

"Yes."

"Watch the papers; he killed Sheriff Swartz of Jennings, Louisiana."

I followed the account and it was true; he had gotten into some trouble over there a few days after our incident and, when the sheriff of Jennings, Louisiana went to arrest him, he shot and killed the sheriff. That's one of the reasons I am glad I didn't have my gun.

From newspaper accounts and from what different colored people who worked for me from time to time told me of the facts, I followed the history of this man throughout his capture, his trial and finally his hanging. After killing Sheriff Swartz, he escaped into the woods around Jennings, a sawmill town. During the time he was sought, according to the stories, he would walk down to the little villages in that part of Louisiana with a Winchester on the crook of his arm and nobody would attempt to arrest him.

I was also told that one day while he was hiding in the woods, a railroad section boss came down the railroad track and flushed a covey of quail. He took his shotgun, flushed them again, shot into the covey and missed. This fellow stepped out of the woods and said, "Do you want some quail?"

"Yes."

He flushed them again and killed two of the birds with his rifle before they got out of rifle range. I do not necessarily believe this story, but it contributes to the fact that I'm glad I didn't engage in a gun battle with him.

Finally, the true facts are that he was hiding in an old abandoned sawmill and some of the colored people of the neighborhood tipped off the sheriff as to his whereabouts. They surrounded this sawmill one night and waited until the moon came up. He came out and the deputy, armed with shotgun and buckshot, yelled for him to put up his hands. Instead of doing so, he "threw up" his Winchester, looking for something to shoot at. He was shot, wounded and captured, then he was hospitalized, cured, tried and sentenced to be hanged. In the meantime, the courthouse burned and he had to be re-sentenced and executed in a different place. He was incarcerated in a different jail, in a different parish and, during that time, he took a piece of glass and tried to cut his throat. They found him before he died, cured him again and finally hanged him. In the account in the paper, before he was hanged he said, "The reason I killed Sheriff Swartz was because he brought a nigger to help arrest me." The statement coincides with the hatred for so-called "niggers" he had expressed to me during the earlier episode.

I still am very thankful that I wanted to see a girl in Beaumont and would have been embarassed to have a big forty-five pistol strapped on while visiting her. I am thankful that the gun was so big I didn't want to carry it under those circumstances. So, I can truthfully say that I owned a forty-five that was so big, it saved my life.

CHAPTER SEVENTEEN

HUNTERS' PARADISE LOST

In the fall of 1914, I owned a team of good trotting mares and a two-seated surrey. I was told by a mutual friend that if I would meet the train at White's Ranch the next morning at ten o'clock, I could earn a few dollars with my rig. Work on the farm was not too urgent and the opportunity to pick up some extra cash appealed to me. The next morning I got an early start and met the train at White's Ranch having no idea as to whom I should meet. When the train stopped, a prosperous looking real estate man got off with an attractive young woman whom he introduced as his daughter, a Beaumont real estate man whom I knew well, and a black male cook with enough fancy groceries to load my carriage.

They told me they wanted to go to Jackson's Ranch six miles across the prairie. They had all kinds of fancy hunting equipment and I thought it was to be strictly a hunting trip. I found later the trip had an entirely different objective. I could not carry the whole load at one trip, so it was decided we would leave the black man with the groceries, carry the rest of the party to the ranch, and I would return for the cook and the groceries.

On Jackson's Ranch was an abandoned house on the prairie ten miles from the nearest neighbor. I made the return trip with the cook and the groceries and was making preparations to return home when the old man came out of the house and said, "Kid, where are you going?" I said, "I am going home." He said, "For God's sake don't leave us down here in this forsaken country." I said, "Alright, I'll stay with you." Then he told me the purpose of the expedition.

Old man John Jackson, the owner of the ranch, had sold his cattle and was permitting these real estate men to divide the ranch into small tracts to sell as farms. The two real estate men in the party were going to hunt for two or three days while they awaited the arrival of their partners. They wanted me to stay and carry them to good hunting grounds.

In 1914, Jackson's Ranch, which covered thousands of acres, was literally a hunter's paradise. Ducks, geese, quail, and prairie chickens abounded. I spent the next couple of days carrying them to the edge of the marsh where ducks and geese were plentiful. I was amazed at the way the twenty-year-old daughter could bring them down with her twenty-gauge gun. The first few days were delightful, especially because the colored man was a superb cook, but when the third partner arrived, all changed. He brought with him two surveyors and plans were made for work to begin.

A young surveyor was to have charge of the surveying crew. His name was Work and he and I in later years were to become very good friends when he became County Surveyor of Chambers County and a very good one too. However, at the time of this incident, the name of "Work" was very inappropriate.

The third real estate partner had brought with him an old engineer, a very fine man by the name of Jenkins. The young engineer had two helpers. Upon the morning of their arrival considerable time was spent in the improvised office which was established in the old ranch house. While they were busy with their plans, I spent the morning under the oak tree in the yard talking to the girl.

When Mr. Jenkins came out he said, "McCall, I have made a contract with these real estate men to survey this large ranch and subdivide it into small farms. It will probably be a year's work. I have another engineering project and cannot be here. I am going to leave the young engineer, Work, in charge and the crew will consist of two other men. I want you to furnish yourself and your team, work with them and haul them from place to place about the ranch." Then he said to me, "The old ranch man has left the corn crib full of corn. You will get four dollars a day for yourself and team, corn for the team, and your food furnished." This sounded good to me, especially when I remembered what a superb cook the old black man was. I accepted the job, but when the hunting party left, they took the cook with them never to return. Left in his place was another black man by the name of Alex Alexander to cook and drive the engineer's car. He may have been a good chauffeur, but he was no cook at all, and the food was terrible.

The surveying began. I had been raised on a farm and was accustomed to rising and having my team hitched and ready early. Young Mr. Work who was the boss, had different ideas. We had to wait for a hearty breakfast to be prepared. The food got worse and worse. One afternoon, however, our work carried us to the edge of the marsh where mallard ducks abounded. We always carried our shot guns with us in the rig. How could we survey land under those circumstances? Well, we didn't. We came in with a large quantity of fat ducks. We were surveyors and it was beneath our dignity to clean and prepare ducks for eating. We threw the whole bunch on the floor of the kitchen.

It is almost impossible for even a poor cook to ruin a good, fat mallard duck, so for two or three days, our food was quite palatable. About the third day, we noticed our ducks had a very unpalatable taste. We got to prowling around the kitchen and found that the cook was cleaning them only as he needed them for the next meal. The odor from that pile of ducks was almost unbearable.

We wanted to kill the cook, but decided against that. Instead, we decided to play a dirty trick. We felt it was time to go to our various homes and get clean clothes and leave the cook alone on the ranch one night. We knew he was afraid of the dark and being alone at night. We left in the morning and spent one night at our homes. We believed we had punished Alex for his bad food by leaving him two days and one night alone. We also knew that Alex was afraid of ghosts. When we got back the second evening and were eating our usual early supper, I said, "Alex, how did you get along while we were gone?" He said, "White folks, I ain't been here. After you left yesterday morning, I got in Mr. Robert's Ford car and spent the two days and night with that nigger over on White's Ranch about ten miles away." I said, "Alex, why did you leave?" He said, "I just ain't gwine to tell you what happened, because I know you white folk don't believe in ghosts." I said, "Oh, yes, Alex, I believe in ghosts. Tell us what happened." "Well, alright, white folks, but you ain't gwine believe it. Yesterday morning, while I was in the kitchen washing dishes, somebody upstairs was throwing chains down that stairway on the back porch and dragging them back, throwing them down and dragging them back."

"Alex, were you scared of those ghosts?", we asked. "Yes, I ran out, got in Mr. Robert's Ford car and spent two days and one night. I just got back here about an hour ago," he said. "Well, don't worry, Mr. Work and I will go upstairs and kill those ghosts," was my reply. We went upstairs, not knowing what he had heard, if anything. We fired a couple of shots with our guns, came down and assured Alex there was nothing more to cause worry. We investigated and found the ghosts. There was a big oak tree at the west end of the ranch house. A tin gutter ran along the west end and when the wind was right, the limbs of the oak tree would rub against the gutter. This had created the sound which Alex believed was the ghost dragging chains.

We still did not feel that we had been fully compensated for the bad food. That night, as was our custom, we had Alex take Mr. Robert's car and drive us the ten miles to White's Ranch to see the train come through. This was the only amusement we had and we often met the White's Ranch boys at the station where we had a hilarious time.

On this night, Alex was driving us back to the Jackson Ranch about ten o'-clock. It must be borne in mind there were no roads other than the two-track wagon trail. The night was very dark and in front of us on Alex's side of the trail a peculiar light began to appear periodically. The nearer we approached, the brighter it would flash. The bearer of the light would not leave the trail. Alex pulled the automobile out of the trail and almost pushed me out of the front seat trying to get away from the object. I cannot blame him much because, as we passed, it turned out to be a horrible looking individual with long hair and beard, puffing on a cigar. At every puff, his face was lit up. We passed him without stopping. I said, "Alex, we didn't kill that ghost after all."

We drove on to the ranch house. It so happened that Mr. Jackson had a large buggy shed. We were so impressed with our status as a surveying crew that we always required our so-called chauffeur to deliver us to the steps of the porch. Work and I got out, but Alex asked the other workmen to hold the garage door open for him so he could put the car away. Work and I realized he was still frightened and took the cue. The ranch house had a long stairway built the length of the long porch. This enabled the cowhands to go to and from their sleeping quarters upstairs and the dining room without disturbing the family. Work and I quickly placed three chairs at the top of the stairway, hid in the dark and, just as Alex stepped on the porch, using surveyors poles, pushed the chairs so that they rolled down the stairway causing a terrible noise. Alex let out a yell, went to his bedroom, and locked the door. Needless to say, our usually late breakfast was unusually late. Twenty years later, when Alex was serving as a cook for a crew of men on my own farm, I told his story and Alex seemed to enjoy it as much as anyone.

What promised to be a delightful winter on Jackson's Ranch came to an end after about six weeks of poor food, short hours, and lots of fun. As was our custom under the supervision of Mr. Work, we ate a late breakfast, drove several miles to where the surveying was to be done and returned to the ranch for a hot lunch. (Carrying a cold lunch was beneath our dignity!) After the noon meal, of course, we had to have a little siesta before returning to our work in the afternoon, and then were back at the ranch for an early supper. This kind of life I was certainly not accustomed to, but it was good while it lasted.

In addition to the evenings of duck hunting, another instance occurred which was not conducive to surveying. Mr. Jackson had a large field of corn on the ranch the year he sold the cattle, and the old corn field was full of quail. One afternoon while we were taking our siesta, Steve, one of the workmen, decided to explore the possibility of there being quail in the corn field. We were awakened by the report of his shot gun, so we grabbed our guns and joined him. The quail were plentiful. How could we survey land under those circumstances?

Now Mr. Roberts, for whom we were working, had been a surveyor in his younger days and had some idea of what a surveying crew should accomplish. He paid us a visit one day, bringing with him Mr. Jenkins, the head surveyor. The two began to check up on our work and spent quite a while in the office. Finally Mr. Jenkins came out to talk to the rest of the crew. He told us that Mr. Roberts had decided to lay the crew off for a few days while he and Mr. Work checked some field notes at the County Court House before we proceeded further. Apparently the plan was to return to the ranch in a few days. Mr. Jenkins told me that in the interim he would use the crew measuring drain ditches in the drainage district near our home. We left the ranch and began the other work which went on for several weeks. Nothing was said about returning to the ranch. During this time, I stayed at home and picked the crew up at Mr. Jenkins's office at Winnie. We measured miles of drainage ditches.

This continued for several weeks with nothing said about returning to the ranch. Finally one morning, when I stopped at the Winnie office to pick up the crew, Mr. Work came up and told me that Mr. Jenkins wanted to see me in the office. Mr. Jenkins was a fine, quiet man, dedicated to his work. Some of his descendants are my best clients and friends. He said, "McCall, Roberts had told me that we would go back to the ranch in a very few days, but he did not order us back to the ranch so I sent him a statement for the work performed. He wrote back that he wanted the work itemized day by day. Mr. Work could not remember what was done on some of the days." My mind quickly reverted to the duck hunting and quail hunting. I said, "Mr. Jenkins, Mr. Work was in charge of this work and I kept no records." We finished the measurements of the drainage ditches, but we never went back to the Jackson Ranch.

Some weeks later after I had acquired another job with my team, I met Mr. Roberts, who had known me well as a farm boy. He stopped his car, came over to my rig and, laughingly, said to me, "McCall, did you ever see anything like that in your life? That fellow, Work, is very improperly named. I have hired another crew and want you to come back to the ranch with your rig." I said, "I am very sorry, Mr. Roberts, I would like to go back, but I have taken another job."

Another incident occurred before we were fired that may be worth mentioning. This was in 1914, a year before the 1915 storm, and because Mr. Jackson had permitted no prairie chicken hunting on his ranch, there were thousands of them. Mr. Roberts told us in the beginning not to shoot prairie chickens. I will digress here a moment to relate the nature, quantity, and quality of a prairie chicken. A grown prairie chicken is about the size of a leghorn hen and the meat is of a very fine quality. The prairie chicken, because of its weight, flies very slowly. In doing so, it makes a very loud noise with its wings, making it a very easy target for huntsmen, which caused it to become practically extinct. I can recall as a child, when we homesteaded on Section 136, there were certain seasons when we almost lived on them. I can recall my mother telling my father, "Quit bringing them home." She was tired of cooking them. They were so thick that one could seldom ride a mile without seeing a covey of them. That condition prevailed on the Jackson Ranch in 1914. The 1915 storm not only destroyed the prairie chickens on Jackson's Ranch, but put an end to the plan to convert the ranch to small farms. It now consists of rice farms and cattle ranching.

Mr. Roberts had planned to build a town at the railroad track which was along the extreme eastern portion of the ranch. During the time before we were fired, he spent a night at the ranch. The next morning he was to show us where to lay out the town site. This involved a trip from the ranch house to the railroad track. He started the crew out in my rig and followed in his Ford. We boys all carried our shot guns. As we were driving along the trail, a nice covey of prairie chickens appeared in the trail ahead of us. Not knowing how close Mr. Roberts was trailing and with my rig making so much noise, Steve, one of the crew, picked up his shot gun and killed a very fine, large prairie chicken. It fell in the trail. I stopped my rig so that Steve could get his prairie chicken. When the noise of the rig ceased, we heard Mr. Roberts' Ford chugging along behind us. Steve said, "Drive on." He did not pick up the chicken. As we looked back, we saw Mr. Roberts get out of his car and pick it up. Nothing was said at the work site. Mr. Roberts beat us back to the ranch by perhaps an hour.

When we sat down to eat there was a big platter of prairie chicken on the table. The cook, of course, first passed the meat to Mr. Roberts. Not being certain whether the prairie chicken had been shot or had died of old age, or worse, he declined, saying "No thanks." I was next at the table and, of course, I did not resist taking a nice, big piece. Then Mr. Roberts said, "Let it come back here; now I know how it died. It's alright this time boys, but don't do it any more."

I suppose the story of the plentifulness of the prairie chicken would not be complete without telling of the time I shot one with my finger. One evening when we were very small boys, my brother and I were driving a herd of cattle along the railroad track. A large covey of prairie chickens flew across the track in front of us. I playfully pointed my finger and said, "Bang." To my surprise one of them dropped dead. He had hit the telephone wire and broken his neck. My mother cooked it for dinner. To show how easily they were killed by huntsmen, I relate this incident. The legislature of Texas, learning how this valuable bird was becoming extinct, passed a law forbidding the killing of prairie chickens. However, about the year 1932 there was an open season one year. Some friends wanted me to take them prairie chicken hunting. We went to a big pasture where prairie chickens could be found. We walked the whole evening without seeing one. I started to walk across a bushy knoll, having given up the hope of finding any. I had my double-barreled shot gun across my shoulder, uncocked, when two chickens flew up in front of me. While they were getting away in that slow, noisy manner, I removed my gun from shoulder, shot both barrels, and killed them both before they got out of range.

I think it only fair to Mr. Work to say that in his later life, he lived up to his name and became a very fine surveyor. He served as County Surveyor of Chambers County for perhaps thirty years and established many land marks which are highly regarded for their accuracy.

Leroy, Alice and Eleric McCall
approximately 1894

Left: Martha Garner McCall, grandmothe[r]
        of Leroy McCall
Below: Sue Green Webb McCall and Davi[d]
        Eleric McCall, parents of Lero[y]
        McCall

Right: John McCall, grandfather of Leroy McCall (photograph is of an oil painting)

Below: David Eleric McCall approximately 70 years old

Above: Members of the Hamshire Baptist Church, 1915
Right: Rice thrashing crew
Below: First lighthouse in Sabine Pass

Right: Eleric McCall, age 70
Center: Alice McCall, ages 22 and 70
Bottom: Lovie McCall Fischer, ages 24 and 63

Leroy McCall, age 25

Leroy McCall, approximately age 40

CHAPTER EIGHTEEN

THE VILLAGE BLACKSMITH

"Under a spreading chestnut-tree
   The village smithy stands;
The smith, a mighty man is he,
   With large and sinewy hands;
And the muscles of his brawny arms
   Are strong as iron bands.

His hair is crisp, and black, and long,
   His face is like the tan;
His brow is wet with honest sweat,
   He earns whate'er he can,
And looks the whole world in the face,
   For he owes not any man ... "
         Henry Wadsworth Longfellow

One of the occupations I attempted to follow before beginning the study and practice of law was that of a village blacksmith.

Perhaps the story of a blacksmith shop does not have any literary value. But since this work is more or less an outline of things as they were three quarters of a century ago, and since a village blacksmith shop would be a curiosity to this generation, it might not be out of place to give it some mention.

About the year 1914, I bought half interest in a blacksmith shop, with a partner by the name of Fred Crenshaw. Fred was wholly illiterate but he had the brawn and the know-how it took to make a good blacksmith. I knew nothing about the trade, but had sufficient money to buy half interest in the shop. It had become a two-man shop and I had the strength necessary to make a good helper and work was plentiful.

I am impressed with the verse of the Village Blacksmith because certainly blacksmithing done in those days required brawn and sinewy hands. And certainly the blacksmith earned the pay he got. I would say for sure that, in our climate, usually more than his brow was wet with honest sweat.

The rice farms required extra heavy wagons which would break down. If the tongue was broken out, we had to replace it. If an axle broke, we had the wood with which to make a new one. If a wheel broke down, we had to re-build it entirely. We had the material and tools and could entirely rebuild a wagon. The tools were crude compared with tools which are available in this day and time. They consisted primarily of forges, anvils, hammers, saws, hatchets, axes, drawing knives, brace and bits and other minor tools all of which were hand tools. Electric or power tools were, of course, unknown to us.

This was just before the advent of the tractors which took the place of the mules on the rice farms. These mules were our responsibility. The work con-sisted largely of keeping them shod, repairing their broken wagons and plows and sharpening plow parts. There was no part of the work that was not hard. Every rice farmer had from four to twelve mules and often more. And they were mules. The rice-farm mule was the largest type of Missouri mule. It took powerful mules to do the rice-field work. The shoeing of a mule required the heating and shaping of the shoe (which was bought from the hardware store), trimming of the mule's hoof, placing the shoe in the right position on the hoof and attaching it with about sixteen nails which were driven from the bottom up through the circle of the edge of the mule's hoof.

The shaping of the shoe, which was Fred's job because he was an expert at the forge and anvil, required it to be heated in the forge and shaped on the anvil to conform to the particular mule's hoof. The shoeing operation, which was my job, required that the foot of the mule be picked up and raised to a position so that the leg could be clasped between the legs of the shoer and held firmly. In this position the shoer would shape the bottom of the hoof off smoothly so the shoe would fit. When the shoe was fitted to conform to the contour of the hoof, it was put on, the nails driven in and clinched on the up-per side of the hoof. Imagine what happened while that operation was taking place if the mule was inclined to be mean or if the shoer would make a mistake and drive his nails in the wrong position so as to strike a tender part of the mule's hoof. Some of these mules were nearly six feet tall and weighed 1200 pounds. In spite of the apparent hazardous work, there were only a few instances when I had to pick myself up from the other side of the blacksmith shop.

CHAPTER NINETEEN

A COUNTRY BOY IN NEW YORK

As I stated in a former chapter, one of the many activities in which I was engaged prior to becoming a lawyer was that of a fig salesman. I acted as plant manager of the fig packing plant until the season was over in the fall. It was then my duty to travel throughout the eastern United States, selling our figs.

I shall never forget my first night in New York City. Imagine a country boy, with limited experience, who had never been over a hundred miles away from home, finding himself in New York City on an important business errand.

We had shipped several carloads of fig preserves to our New York broker, who was selling them on a commission basis and making us monthly returns. The monthly returns ceased and we did not hear from him. Part of my duty in New York was to contact him, collect what I could and place the account in the hands of another broker. When I contacted him, he admitted that he had gone broke and that he had sold a quantity of figs for which he owed us twenty-two hundred dollars. He said that he was unable to pay us more than two hundred dollars and would have to give us a note for the two thousand. There seemed no other way to settle with him so I accepted his check for two hundred dollars and his note for two thousand.

I had no idea if the check was any good. His offices were on Wall Street and only about a block from the bank on which the check was drawn. I had no hope of cashing the check, believing it was not good, but I walked into the bank. It was a cold day and I was wearing a big overcoat. I endorsed the check, and passed it into the teller's window. He looked at it and motioned to someone in the lobby. The man in the lobby approached me from behind, turned my overcoat collar down and asked the teller what the name was on the check. When he heard my name he said, "O.K.", turned and walked away. The teller cashed the check. I said, "That's pretty good. I really did not know the laundry mark was on my overcoat." He said, "Yes, the overcoat fit you, the laundry mark shows it to be the same as the name on the check and that's the best method of identification." I had never heard of that before. I had no hope of cashing a check in that bank, being a perfect stranger.

By then, it was noon on a Saturday and, as no further business could be attended to until Monday morning, I decided to see New York. I took the Eastside elevated train and rode as far as it went. Then I walked across the island and took the Westside back as far as Central Park, got off and walked all over Central Park. I was only thirty-three years old and strong as a mule.

Before leaving home, I attended a party given by my sister and some other school teachers who had been to New York. They told me by all means to visit Earl Carol's Vanities. That was a theater with some notoriety because a short time before that, Earl Carol had been indicted because he had put on a show where one of his actresses took a bath in a tub of champagne on the stage. While this caused him criminal prosecution, the publicity made him rich. Everyone from out of town who had read this wanted to go to Earl Carol's show. Finally the night came I was to go and, being a country boy, I was a little early. While I was sitting there waiting for the show to begin, a man came out on the stage and announced that if any young men wanted to dance they could come to the back of the stage and be introduced to some of the girls and could dance on the stage. I thought "Wow, what an opportunity. I'll go back and tell the girls that I not only went to Earl Carol's show but I danced on the stage." I was introduced to a girl and we danced. I know I stepped on her toes miserably and was a very poor dancing partner but, after all, I had danced on Earl Carol's stage.

After the show I started back to my hotel room and, at that time, they had what were called jitney dancing studios. I don't think they reached the southern towns but New York was full of them. There was a stairway going up to the second floor advertising dancing. I went up. Well, you bought ten tickets for a dollar. There was a whole bunch of girls in a little enclosure and you could pick out any one you wanted. I started dancing. When the music had gone about three minutes, she would tear off one of your tickets and you could either dance with her or someone else. You didn't get much dancing for your dollar. However, I danced there until I was tired and then started back to my hotel.

I got down to Times Square where there was a man announcing the fact that the sight-seeing bus was making its last tour for the night and we could visit Grant's Tomb, China Town, and other places of interest for a dollar. It was then almost midnight but I said, "OK, I'll make a night of it," so I crawled on. Very few people were on the bus and I sat immediately behind the man with the trumpet who announced the sights and we fell into conversation. He asked me where I was from and I said that I was from Texas. He said this was his last run that night and he asked if I would like to see some of New York's night life. I said, "No, I didn't drink and I didn't gamble and I wasn't interested in women." I thought I would go back to my hotel room and go to sleep. He said that I didn't have to drink anything, we could just go to this place he had in mind and I could buy a soft drink and sandwich and see what goes on. I said, "OK". He said that he would be back in ten minutes, after putting up his bus. I said I had to go to the hotel to attend to a little errand. The hotel was three blocks away and I guess I was a little apprehensive because I checked the considerable amount of money I had on me with the hotel clerk and took only five dollars. You see, I didn't know what I was getting into.

I met him as agreed and we walked about three blocks on Seventh Street and down a stairway. At the end of the stairway, there was a door with a little hole in it. He put his mouth in the hole and said, "Let me in; it's Mike."

This was in prohibition time. The doorkeeper opened the door and we entered a hallway. At the other end of the hall, about sixty feet away, was a little stairway going up to a room that turned out to be a barroom the like of which I had seen before prohibition in Beaumont, Texas. From the barroom one entered a big dance hall where there were a lot of people. Some were sitting around tables drinking and some were dancing. We sat at a table. A waitress soon came and we ordered sandwiches and a cola. The check was brought and I picked it up. It was for $3.50. Of course, it was about three times what it should have been, but that was alright; I was seeing night life in New York. We sat there a few minutes. Finally two girls came and flopped themselves down at our table. We got to talking and one of them, addressing me, said "Big Boy, buy us some drinks."

I said, "No, I don't buy drinks."

She suggested we dance, so we danced a little while and sat down again. She immediately waved to the waiter to come over and ordered four bottles of wine and a bottle of champagne. I still did not fall to what was taking place. The wine and champagne were immediately opened. One of the girls poured some champagne in my glass. I don't know why I did it but I had never tasted champagne or any other liquor in my life and thought I would see what it was like. To me it tasted like kerosene oil. I think the peculiar taste

90

started me to thinking and wondering what was going on. I said to the girl, "Who's paying for these drinks?"

"You are, Big Boy," she said.

"No, I told you, I was buying no drinks."

"Well, now you'll have to."

I said, "No."

I picked up my check for $3.50, walked over to the bartender standing by the cash register and said, "Listen, this is what I bought and this is what I'm paying for. I did not order those drinks and I am not paying for them."

"You'll have to. You're going to get us into trouble. They are going to have to be paid for," he said. "No," I said.

I threw down my $3.50 on his counter, walked over to where I had hung my overcoat and put it on. He followed me to the little stairway. I was scared. I got my overcoat on and started down the hall toward the door keeper. I looked him straight in the eye and pushed my overcoat back as though I was going for a gun. Incidentally, I didn't have a gun. If I had had a gun, I would have been too scared to use it.

I think they couldn't figure me out. I was wearing pretty good clothes and a western hat. Anyway, to my great relief, as I approached the door keeper, the bartender behind me said, "Oh, hell, let him go." And go I did. I left there a wiser and a sadder boy. I know now, that I was not supposed to get out of there alive; I was supposed to wind up in the Hudson River.

I've never tasted champagne again and do not know whether that kerosene taste is a natural taste of champagne or the taste of some dope they had put in it. I do know that it was a good thing that I was not a drinking man or I might not have been here to tell this story.

CHAPTER TWENTY

EDUCATION UNDER DIFFICULTIES

Since this narrative is based upon facts and does not contain enough history, philosophy, tragedy or comedy to make it worth reading otherwise and has degenerated into an autobiography, I think it only fair to myself and the readers (if any), that I give an account of my education.

Even if it were possible in this era, I would not recommend that a young person allow his course of education to follow that which mine followed. I think I have missed, more than anything else in life, the fellowship of former schoolmates which other persons have enjoyed in later life.

As I stated before, we returned to Sabine Pass when I was five years of age and remained there for five years, returning to Hamshire in the year 1902. During our five years at Sabine Pass, when I became eight years of age, my mother thought I should go to school, but did not want me to go to the public school, as she had heard the children were very rough. Since my mother was a very religious woman, she did not want me to learn to curse. She sent me to a private school which, I suppose, was something like a kindergarten. It was run by a woman by the name of Mrs. Pratt. She was a nice old lady but I do not remember learning anything in her school. It lasted three months, then her health required her to close it. The next school season would be the school year of 1901 and 1902 when my mother's burning desire that we have an education overcame her fear and we were sent to the public school at Sabine Pass. At that time it was a one-room wooden school building. The teacher who began the term was Mrs. Brad Johnson. It is interesting to know that a few years ago, when she became eighty years of age, she sent for me to come to her home in Port Arthur to write her will. Her health caused her to give up the school in the middle of the term and a very fine woman by the name of Stella Wilber, who incidentally was a sister of the late Charles Wilber and the aunt of the several Wilber men who live in Hamshire at this time, came to Sabine Pass and completed the term. She later married Ben Pipkin, and I believe she was the mother of Bruce Pipkin, a very fine man and a ranchman who still lives in Hamshire.

I do not recall exactly what grade I was in at Sabine Pass, but it was probably about the fifth grade. My brother, who was two years older, attended the same school. The school only took them through the seventh grade and, while that was the only year he ever went to public school in his life, he graduated and was valedictorian of his class. Our mother, a well-educated woman, bought the necessary school books and taught us behind the kitchen stove while she was attending her household duties. I never learned much that year in school, in fact, I was too scared. However, as I recall, I completed a full nine-month term. We moved to Hamshire the first part of August 1902, and the school house where I attended classes had some history which is perhaps worth telling. I do not know the history of the building prior to 1872, but at that time the little one-room school house, approximately 20 by 30 feet in size, was located on the Arceneaux place, which is now the Junker Spencer's place, about two miles east of Hamshire. The school house was where Junker Spencer's cattle pens are now on the road from Hamshire to the Stringtown settlement. Of course there were no roads in those days; we just traveled across the prairie.

I know the school house was there at that time because my father attended school there at least one term. He had been attending school in Sabine Pass taught by a woman his parents thought was a very excellent teacher. Moise Broussard employed this teacher, whose name I do not remember, to teach in the little one-room school house that he had provided for his children and those of his neighbors. So my father was sent to live in the home of Mr. Broussard and attend school with his children. Dad told us he did not recall much that he learned in the school house, but he did recall very vividly learning to rope calves and ride horses with the Broussard boys.

In 1902, before the school began in September, my father and Edgar Carruthers, who were school trustees, decided the school should be moved to a point near the center of the neighborhood. It was moved to a position on the Aubey land, almost across the road from what is now the Melancon place where the big oak trees are, a mile and a half east of Hamshire. The teacher that year was Miss Lovina Scoffield, who came from the Hankamer area where she was raised. I was still in the fifth grade, but I didn't learn much; I

93

was still scared. All the other students were much older than I, being ten years of age and a very timid child. The school term started in September but I had to quit at the Christmas holidays because of eye trouble and not being able to read without having very severe headaches. My mother scraped up enough money to send me to Beaumont to an eye specialist, who said that my trouble was an astigmatism and I was growing too fast. He furnished some glasses which I think cost $18.00. I don't think they did me any good and they didn't last long because glasses did not fit into my scheme of life. After I had them about two weeks, an unruly horse carried me under an oak tree and that was the end of the glasses. There was no money to buy another pair. That suited me fine since I didn't like school anyway; the only ambition I had at that time was to be a cowboy. My mother finally decided that that would be my fate and gave up on my formal education.

The condition of my eyes prevented me from studying or reading for many years. During this time I believe I became an excellent farm hand and cowboy. We had to make our living from our cattle and from the soil. My brother and I would occasionally get a job working on a rice farm at harvest time. The wages were $1.00 a day and dinner and the hours were from daylight until dark. We did not mind that; we were accustomed to it. Finally, when I got my growth at about nineteen years of age, my eyes improved. In fact, my eye trouble was entirely gone, and now at eighty-five years of age, I think I have remarkably good eyes. I have used Kress glasses to read with for the past thirty years, but my distant vision is as good as ever. I can shut one eye and drive to Dallas and shut the other and drive back safely as far as vision is concerned. I think that is remarkable considering my early eye experience.

There was no social life in the community, in fact, I never went to a party or dance until I was 23 years of age. I didn't even own a dress suit, just overalls and work clothes. When my mother learned I could read again, she encouraged home study. My brother, who was a regular "book-worm," always had books on hand. I think I got more inspiration for an education from the Galveston Daily News than from any other source. At that time, we took the paper and, as I recall, the editor was named A. H. Beall. His editorials were something wonderful. I remember that I devoured them all and everything else I could get my hands on. It must be borne in mind that the only time we had for reading was Sundays and nights.

The winter of 1912 and 1913 was the worst I have ever known in this country. It rained all winter; we lost our crop and a great many cattle, but I think it was the most profitable period of my life because I spent the entire winter reading. My brother had acquired a set of books called Ridpath's History of the World in eight volumes and I read that. There was also a book I read called the Chemistry of Plant and Animal Life. I also remember a two-volume work called Brand's Iconoclast.

Somehow I acquired the desire for an education. That winter, my brother went to Mexico to work for my uncle on a rice farm. I was running the farm with the help of my father, whose health was bad at that time. With the help of the cattle, we made our living raising Irish potatoes, sweet potatoes, sugar cane, corn and vegetables. We had no land suitable for rice. In the paper I saw an advertisement from the LaSalle Correspondence School of Law in Chicago and I subscribed for the course. At that time the requirement of the bar association in Texas was the completion of sixteen subjects in law and an examination on them. I began studying law by correspondence and, when my brother returned from Mexico, I had completed five of the sixteen subjects. It is no easy task to follow a plow twelve hours a day and concentrate on law at night. The revolution drove my brother out of Mexico for the second time. The first time he had been farming and the second time had been working in the oilfield. While in the oilfield, he sent all of his money home and, unknown to him, I saved considerable cash. When he came back and found me studying, he said to me, "What are you doing with all these books?" I said I was studying law by correspondence. He said, "I would like to study law, but not that way." I had kept up with the situation and knew that there was one law school in the United States that offered enough law in one year to pass the bar examination. Remember, no previous law study or any education for that matter, was necessary. In fact, in the early days in Texas, to become a lawyer an applicant took an examination which was given by three lawyers appointed by a local Court. If he passed, he became a lawyer. It has been rumored that many times the examining lawyers took him no further than the bar across the street and if he could drink more than the examining lawyers, he was qualified. I don't know how true that was; I know we had some fine lawyers in Texas in the early days and some of them were highly qualified drinkers.

The law school I had in mind was a branch of Columbia University in Lebanon, Tennessee. In September, my brother went to Lebanon with enough money to complete the nine-month course. Many Texas men had been to that school, including the famous Joe Bailey of two generations past. During this term, there were many Texas boys in the Lebanon school. They heard it rumored that Texas was going to pass a law requiring pre-law education in order to be qualified to take the bar examination. My brother heard the rumor and came back during the Christmas holidays, and studied law at home night and day and took the bar examination in June, passing with honors. At that time the examination was given by three lawyers in each Civil Appeals

Judicial District. Appointed by the Supreme Court, they were highly qualified men.

My brother and I had made an agreement that he would finish first. I thought that was right since he was older than I. He was then to come back and run the farm while I attended law school. About the time he finished, World War I was underway so it was useless to plan to go to law school. I continued to farm and he returned to the oilfield. Since I was a farmer and he was an oilfield worker, we were in the so-called second draft. I was called up in the spring of 1918 for a physical examination and passed in good shape. When they learned I had considerable crops growing, they told me to go back, harvest my crops and report again November 1. So I harvested my crops and went back November 1, took another physical and was told to report for duty on December 1.

I came back to the farm and decided to continue to work until I had to go. Due to the war, the hay market was fine and even the frost stayed off late that year. I was cutting and bailing hay from the same land we had cut hay in 1902. I was shipping it to Beaumont and getting a good price. On November 11, 1918, I was mowing hay on the area which is now my pecan orchard. My father ran a little store at Hamshire in which he had the post office. There was no television and radio; the only news people got was through the newspaper. Several boys in the Hamshire area were in the army and, of course, their families were very concerned. Every morning a T-Model truck brought the bread out from Beaumont to the store and also brought the morning paper. This particular morning when the bread truck stopped, I heard all the car horns around there blowing. The bread truck soon went down the highway past near where I was working, blowing his horn all the way. I knew something had happened so I hitched my team to the fence and walked back to the store and learned that the armistice had been signed and the war was over. I went back to making hay.

By this time my brother had married and started a family and it seemed that my law ambitions had come to an end. Much water went under the bridge from 1918 until 1930. Besides farming, I worked in the oilfield, punched cattle, worked as a longshoreman in Galveston, ran a blacksmith shop and finally became engaged in the real estate business with the Koch Land Company. In June, 1923, I married one of the sweetest women I ever knew. She died in childbirth in January, 1925. The child was lost also. Two years later I married my second wife, who died in 1975 and was a very remarkable woman. She was at that time the School Superintendent of Jefferson County, Texas, and very well educated. Her education was a great inspiration and help to me. By that time, I had become involved in the fig-packing business.

By 1930, the business had failed and the depression was underway. The depression of the '30's is something which I hope this generation will not have to experience. There was no money, no work and no business. My wife had a very good position for those days and we were living quite well. Without her help I could not have made it. We were living on the farm and she was teaching school. I saw in the Beaumont Enterprise that there was a night law school organized in Beaumont. It had been going on about two months when I discovered it. I expressed the desire to go to the school and she encouraged me. I attended for three months but found that, as far as I was concerned, they were plowing old ground. All of this previous law work came back to me and I did not have to study. I made up my mind to quit the school and start studying night and day as my brother had done because there was another rumor that the law would be changed. The following June I took the bar examination in Austin. It was tough. Eighty-five percent of the three hundred that took it failed.

The hardest work I have done was preparing for that examination. It was given in the House of Representative rooms in the Capitol building in Austin. We were examined in sixteen subjects over a four-day period. Again it was reported that the law was about to be changed requiring pre-law education, which I did not have. At the time of the June 1932 examination, I had not completed the sixteen subjects upon which we were to be examined. However, I decided to take the examination and pass as many as I could. A rule then allowed one to take a second time the examinations only on the subjects in which one had failed.

Jack Voiles, who later became a successful lawyer in Port Arthur and who was in the Beaumont Law School when I quit, upon learning that I was going to take the bar examination, also quit the school and went with me to Austin. There was a fine old woman in Austin at that time by the name of Sanborn, who conducted a night school preparing applicants for the bar. Mrs. Sanborn's school started three weeks before the examinations. We had three weeks to cram courses and one week of examinations. It was four weeks, night and day, of hard work.

When we went to Austin, Jack and I had brought along all the text books we had. We got a room in the old Capitol Hotel and started studying. We would start studying at four a.m. At eight a.m. we went across the street for breakfast, then returned to study until noon. Immediately after lunch there was study again until eight p.m., class time. After class, we returned to our room to study until midnight.

After twenty-one days of this grueling schedule, came four days of examination. Four subjects were taken each day and the answers written in long hand.

When I left the Capitol Building on that Thursday evening of the fourth week, I knew I had failed all of the subjects, but was so tired, I didn't care. My wife and daughter, Mary Sue, then four years of age, came to Austin in the car and took me home.

That "don't care" feeling was only temporary. At once I began studying night and day to be ready to take the examination again in December. We were told earlier, as mentioned above, we could take the examination the second time on any subject failed in the first effort. There were so many taking the examinations in June, it was November 15 before we got any report on our efforts and then, only the first twelve of the sixteen subjects. To my surprise, I passed all of the twelve subjects. I was sure then that I could pass the other four subjects in December. I made up my mind to get ready.

On December first, I went to Beaumont, rented an office in the old Pearlstein Building for $15.00 per month. It would cost at least $190.00 today. When I got home that night, my license was in the mail! I had passed the other four subjects.

CHAPTER TWENTY-ONE

WHY DID I STUDY LAW?

One may well ask, as I have asked myself many times, "Why did you undertake to become a lawyer after you were forty years of age?" I'm not quite sure of the proper answer. It may have been because I never failed to serve on a jury from the time I was 21 until I was 40 and I became fascinated by the courtroom. It may have been that, like many other country boys who worked hard, I believed practicing law was a better and easier way to make a living. No greater mistake was ever made. I found when I became a lawyer, hard work really began. I must have recognized the necessity for hard work before I took the bar examination for I recall an answer I gave to one of the questions. The question was: What is a lawyer's duty to his client? I gave the usual expected answer: "Honesty, candor, dedication to the client's case," and one or two other stereotypic responses. To them I added: "Perhaps the greatest duty is industry. Client's rights are found in hundreds of law books including statutes, textbooks and court reports. Those rights cannot be determined except by a tremendous amount of hard work." I got 99 on the subject, Legal Ethics. Perhaps the old judge that graded the paper knew well what I had learned.

I soon found a country lawyer did not choose his work. He cannot be a specialist. Today he may be defending a traffic ticket and tomorrow, be probating a will involving a million-dollar estate. He may be involved in a law suit affecting millions of dollars worth of oil property or defending a person accused of rape, murder, fondling or arson. In my forty-three years of practice, I have been involved in many varied matters. I think it safe to say I have handled at least a thousand divorces.

In Southeast Texas, many contests have arisen involving water rights. I have represented many persons in the last forty years in cases involving water rights. It so happened that many of the farmers I represented farmed a lot of rice. Rice needs a lot of water. The water is not only obtained from large irrigation canals, but those farmers who have acquired land near a bayou water their rice with individual pumps under riparian (riparian is the ownership of land adjacent to a bayou, river or lake) and permit rights. Many controversies have arisen and I have enjoyed an interesting and lucrative practice before the Water Rights Commission of the State of Texas and in the local courts. I recall an incident many years ago when I filed a suit in the District Court against an upper riparian user, on behalf of a lower riparian user. The upper riparian user was accused of damming the bayou and cutting off the water, destroying the rights of the lower landowner. This case was to be tried by a very fine district judge, now long deceased. He had quite a sense of humor and, since I had been before him on other occasions battling over water rights, he jokingly said to me when I walked in the courtroom, "LeRoy, how long you gonna be involved in these water rights cases?" I said, "Judge, I cannot answer that question. But the best answer I can give you is to quote to you what I read last night in a Supreme Court decision in making preparation for this trial. The old Supreme Court judge who was trying a water-rights case made the remark in his decision, that 'water had been important to mankind, and there had been controversies over it ever since the dawn of history and that it would continue to be important to mankind, and there would continue to be controversies over it up until the last syllable of human history is written.' Now Judge, I will not be involved that long, but that's the best answer I can give you."

In this area, which has in the last thirty or forty years become an oil-producing country, many controversies also arise over oil rights. My son and I, mostly my son, recently completed a case involving $300,000 worth of oil royalty. The history of this is worth narrating because the legal aspects may be interesting to the layman. In addition, I believe this story will show what a country lawyer's work is like.

Our client, a very fine young farmer, wanted to purchase a half section of land, 320 acres, to add to his large farming operation. The land belonged to people in the North. He went to them and negotiated for the purchase of the land at a very fair price. However, the owners said, "We will not sell this land at that price unless we can sell half of the mineral rights under it for $9,000. We need more money than you're paying for the land." Our client was unwilling and unable to buy the mineral rights at that time. He contacted a man he knew in Chicago who was buying minerals in the Beaumont area and told him of the opportunity he had. The Chicago man said that he would take the minerals at that price. Our client had two deeds made by the owners and sent them to the bank in Beaumont. One was to be delivered to him upon payment for the surface, and the other one was to be delivered to the buyer of the minerals upon payment for the rights. Before the deeds reached the bank in Beaumont the man in Chicago changed his mind. Our client could not acquire the surface without buying the minerals, and he did not have the money nor desire to buy them. He came to me with this dilemma. I said, "Don't let those deeds be sent back by the bank. Borrow the money, and buy the minerals. That land will be worth as much to you for a farm as you're paying for both the surface and the minerals." He did and acquired the surface and one-half of all mineral rights.

Some years before, the owners in the North had made a lease to an oil producer. Two wells had been drilled on the land and were productive for several years. At the time my client bought the land these wells had gone dry. He contacted the oil operators, asked them to move their equipment and clean up the land so he could farm it. A controversy arose, but, as a result of the contact a new lease was made by our client. Two new wells, which became very productive, were dug. Twenty years before this transaction, the owners had sold what is called "twenty-year term royalty," which simply meant that the buyers of the royalty would get the royalty on the production for twenty years and for as long thereafter as production continued. After twenty years, there being no production, the royalty rights would terminate. The persons who bought this royalty were royalty dealers. They operated by buying a producing royalty, contacting many persons who were inclined to gamble on oil royalties and sold small interests to them, retaining some for themselves. In this instance, the royalty was payable to about forty people all over the country. A few of the larger holders learned of this new production and that the owners had leased to the same producers. Believing that there was conspiracy to let production cease and the old term royalty lapse, they brought a suit for their royalty. We represented our original client, who had bought the surface and half of the royalty with the people in the North retaining the other half. The suit involved a contest between our clients and persons who bought interest in the "twenty year term royalty." Since all of the many holders of interests in the royalty were not party to the original suit, the court required us to bring in all of the many owners of the "twenty year term royalty." Believe it or not, among the others we had to sue were Amos and Andy, the radio comedians of several years past. Another owner we found in England, and it was a task to get proper legal service on both Amos and Andy, who were then travelling in Europe, and the man in Eng-

101

land.

When a suit arises over the ownership of royalty, the oil producer simply holds the royalty payments until the suit is determined and the court tells them whom to pay. Having been engaged in such matters before and, knowing that the major companies will always have the money available when the matter is determined, we gave no thought to impounding this royalty money. One day the ladies who work in the title office my son and I maintain in Anahuac, Texas were laughing about a divorce decree, a copy of which they had been required to make. One of them said to the other, "I sure would like to have been that man's wife. Looka here. She got a million-dollar property settlement." I said, "Let me see that." The husband involved in the divorce case was a small, independent oil producer and was the man who was holding the money. I said, "Let me think here. If he gets married again and has another experience like that, he will be broke and all of our money will be gone." As a result of that little incident in that title office, I got busy and had the royalty money impounded. Ninety days after it was impounded, the man was broke. Because of the little amusement the women were having over the divorce decree, our clients and the other interested persons were saved several hundred thousand dollars.

CHAPTER TWENTY-TWO

HOW LAWYERS ARE MADE

I had been involved in many things. I was first a cow puncher, a farm-hand, a blacksmith, a justice of the peace, a deputy sheriff, a longshore worker, a traveling salesman, the manager of a fig-preserving plant, a real-estate dealer, an assistant postmaster, a restaurant owner, a depot agent, and the manager of a Farmers Cooperative Marketing Association. Not overly successful at any of these, I became a lawyer.

I have often said, perhaps jokingly and perhaps more or less seriously, much to the displeasure of my young lawyer friends, that when a man is not worth much for anything else, they make of him a lawyer. This brings to mind a story. Over 20 years ago, I maintained my office in Beaumont and, because I couldn't get farming out of my blood, I maintained quite a farming operation, at considerable financial loss, on the land I then and now own, a part of the old Section 136 at Hamshire. The law practice was not as de-manding and active as now. I would sneak away from Beaumont and some-times spend two or three days on the farm, working with the farmhands. On one occasion I was in the cow lot (I had a good many cattle), helping the farmhands load manure on the two-horse wagon to fertilize a melon patch. While engaged in this operation, two men drove up in an automobile. One was a judge before whom I had a case pending and the other, a lawyer. I do not remember the purpose of their visit, but perhaps it was to remind me of something I had neglected. One of them said, "Mac, what in the world are you doing out here with this?" I said, "Boys, I'll tell you a story which per-haps will illustrate this situation."

"Many years ago, beyond your recollection, but not beyond mine, there were no automobiles such as you are driving, to carry lawyers to the country to visit clients. These trips had to be made in a livery rig. There were livery stables with rigs of two trotting horses and a surrey, which carried people to the country. During that period of time, there were two young lawyers who wanted to consult a client far out in the country. The only way they could reach him was to go to the livery stable, hire a livery rig and be driven to the client's home. It so happened that they were short-handed at the livery stable. The owner had to send an old, old Irishman by the name of Pat to drive the rig. It was a very cold day, raining and sleeting. Old Pat had to sit on the front seat unprotected from the weather while the two lawyers in the back were well-protected and wrapped in robes. The lawyers very unwisely decided to kid old Pat about his situation. 'Pat, you're mighty old to be out in this kind of weather.' He said, 'Yes, I'm too old to be out in this kind of weather.' The other said, 'Pat, what do they do with you boys around the livery stable when you get too old to drive in bad weather?' Pat answered, 'Well, when we get to where we're 'no count' and can't be trusted, they put us to feeding and harnessing horses.' Perhaps they had carried the kidding far enough, but the other spoke up again and said, 'Pat, when you get too old for that, then what?' Pat said, 'Well, young fella, when we get to where we can't be trusted to feed and harness the horses, they put us to cleaning out the stalls.' They should not have carried it any further, but the other one spoke up, 'Pat, when you get too old for that, then what?' Pat, being by then pretty much aggravated, stopped his horses, 'Whoa!,' and turned around, 'Young man, when we get so no count we ain't fit to shovel manure around the barn anymore, they send us up town and make lawyers of us.'"

I said to my judge and lawyer friends, "Boys, the time will come when I won't be good for this anymore, so I'll be back up there with you."

CHAPTER TWENTY-THREE

CASE WON ON THE TEN COMMANDMENTS

Regardless of the reason that impelled me to take up law, I will say I have no regrets. In fact, law is full of matters of deep human interest and a country lawyer's work is so varied it never gets dull. It has its sad features, its happy features, its depressing moments and its exhilarating moments. There's nothing more exhilarating than, after having worked on a case for days and having argued your case to the jury, to have the jury return a verdict in your favor. On the other hand, there's nothing more depressing than to have the jury come back and return a verdict against you. This is especially true if you were depending upon a contingent fee to pay your office rent and your grocery bill. If a lawyer tells you he never lost a lawsuit, he's either lying, or has tried very few.

In meditating over past courtroom experiences, many interesting incidents come to mind.

I will never forget the case I won on the Ten Commandments. To relate this properly, I must give some information on what we call our limitation laws in Texas. If this is boring, I have to tell you that a lot of research of law is boring unless you just naturally like it. Also, if a lawyer reads this, he may disagree with my interpretation of the law.

When Texas first became a state, the legislature passed what we call a "ten-year limitation statute." Briefly, it rules that if a person takes possession of land and uses and claims it for ten years adversely to everyone else he becomes the owner regardless of who had the record or deed title. This has become very unpopular with the average jury in recent years, and I have been somewhat provoked that the legislature has not amended it over the long period of time. The statute states if one has possession of land, claiming and using same for ten years prior to the time a suit for the title is brought, the record owner cannot win. That's not exactly the wording of the statute because I do not have it before me, but the important point is the word "claim." I believe if the legislature would add "claim in good faith" the thing would make sense.

The reason for the enactment of that statute at the beginning of the history of Texas was that many settlers came to Texas in the early days under grants from the Mexican government before the Texas Revolution, under patents from the Republic of Texas and, later, under patents from the State of Texas. These settlers who were given land in the early days had no way of knowing exactly where their land lines were. Surveyors were very scarce and expensive and the average settler could not afford to have the land surveyed and stakes set at his corners. Some of it was such a wilderness, it was impossible to survey. This I know from our own experience. When my father acquired Section 136 by patent from the State of Texas in 1895, he certainly could not afford a surveyor even if one had been available. He wanted to fence this section. He knew where the northeast corner was because the adjoining section had been surveyed and the stakes set and he knew the northwest corner was one mile due west. So, what did he do? Knowing that a mile was 5,280 feet, he tied a white rag around the spoke of his wagon wheel, measured the distance around the wagon wheel, put a pocket compass on the wagon seat and had my uncle drive due west. He counted the revolutions of the wheel and did the calcuating. Believe it or not, thirty years later, when I had that section surveyed and fenced, that northwest corner was only eight feet off. But what did eight feet amount to at that time, since the land only cost him $3.00 an acre?

The purpose of the statute was to protect a settler who fenced in the land he considered his and occupied it for ten years. No one could take it away from him. When this matter first reached the courts and this ten-year statute was attacked as being unwise, the courts said it was a good law because the settlers would feel secure in their homes if they were allowed to keep what they took possession of, believing it was their own. Millions of dollars worth of land have been "stolen" under this statute. You can fence in anybody's land, use it and occupy it for ten consecutive years without the knowledge of the owner. You can then bring a suit to clear your title, take the witness stand looking honest and get the jury to believe you claimed it for ten years. This is true whether you had claimed it in good faith or started with the intent to steal it.

Twenty years ago, I was employed by a man who had record title to seven acres of land valued at about $20,000. Since he was a non-resident and had not visited the land in recent years, he did not know that during the depression when land was almost worthless an individual had fenced in his acreage along with other land. My client had an opportunity to sell his land, drove out to show it to the prospective buyer, and found it had been enclosed by a fence for many years. He went to the man who had it fenced and asked him about it. He said, "Oh, that's my land. I've had it fenced in for thirty years. It's mine and I'm not going to give it up!" I sued the man who had the land fenced.

The trial lasted for three days. It included a great amount of testimony from both sides. The man who claimed the land took the stand looking perfectly honest and told the jury he had been using, cultivating and claiming this land for thirty years. There was no one to deny that. We finished the evidence and prepared the charge.

Such cases are submitted to the jury on special issues. The Court asks the jury to answer certain questions and tells the jury their answers to the questions will constitute the verdict. The key question in this case was, "Did this man claim this land?" The jury argument was to start the next morning. I woke in the middle of the night wondering how I was going to persuade the jury that the man didn't claim the land when he said he did. I knew the jury was composed of some very good people, some being good church members. The next morning when I began the argument, I said, "Ladies and gentlemen of the jury, the Court has asked you to answer several questions. One of them and, I think, the most important one is, 'Did the defendant claim this land?' Now, ladies and gentlemen, claim is a state of mind. Nobody can say a person does or does not claim anything. It is a mental attitude in regard to a matter. But, I say to you, this defendant's mental attitude toward that land was expressed (so far as we know) six thousand years ago; it is in the tenth verse of the fifth chapter of Deuteronomy. It is the Tenth Commandment, 'Thou shalt not covet.' Now ladies and gentlemen, the mental attitude toward that land was not of claim, but of covet." I proceeded to give Webster's dictionary definition of the two words, "claim" and "covet." The lawyer on the other side, still a very good friend of mine and a man whose friendship I value highly, jumped up and objected to the fact that I used the Bible in my argument. The very fine old judge, who is now deceased said, "Well, I'll let Brother McCall quote the Bible a little if he wants to." I was allowed to continue with that line of argument. The jury retired and was back in five minutes and said the defendant did not claim the land.

I say I won that law suit on the Ten Commandments and every time I meet

107

my good friend, the defendant's lawyer, at different courthouses around the country, he doesn't fail to tell everybody present how wrong the good old judge was in permitting me to quote the Bible.

CHAPTER TWENTY-FOUR

CASE LOST

As I sit here in my room on the seventh floor of the old Jean LaFitte Hotel in Galveston where I have come to concentrate on this work in quiet surroundings, I look at the courthouse two blocks away and am reminded of a case I tried there many years ago. This one we lost and should have lost because we found, after being in the trial a week, the facts were against us. However, sometimes the cases you lose are just as interesting and just as educational as the ones you win.

The heirs of Shanghai Pierce, the early ranchman involved in the trail drives to Kansas, instituted a suit against the heirs of a man named Dunman. Before the Civil War, Dunman had acquired a league of land on the Bolivar Peninsula, west of High Island. There was a bad break in the Pierce chain of title and suit was brought against all the Dunman heirs to clear the defects in the title. When the Dunman heirs were served with citations in the case some of the remote heirs of Dunman came to see me about defending the suit, thinking perhaps they could win some land. I told them there had been so many heirs and such a long division that, if they won the case, they would have so little it was not worth the expense and trouble. Their chances of winning were remote. I turned them down at first, but a lawyer friend of mine in an adjoining city was approached by some of the heirs and, collectively, they had enough to make the defense of the suit worthwhile. He persuaded me to join forces and defend this suit. The original patentee had died unmarried and left several brothers and sisters. We represented the remote heirs of one of the sisters. My associate's theory was that the alleged conveyance signed by the sister a hundred years ago was a forgery. If he was correct, our clients still had their interest.

His theory of the forgery was based on the fact that the deed had been signed by the marks of Susan, the sister of the deceased original patentee, and by Reuben, Susan's husband. However, only a few years before and a few years after making these marks, Susan and Rueben had signed deeds by signature rather than by mark. The theory, of course, was that this deed was signed by mark so that the forgery would never be identified. At the present time, when a deed is filed in the clerk's office, a photostat is made and the copy is recorded in a book, The deed is sent back to the grantee. However, in those days, the deeds were copied in longhand in the record book, and the deed sent back to the grantees. When they were copied, it was indicated whether the signature was by mark or by signature, but the actual signature of the makers of deeds was not reflected on the record book; they were copied in the handwriting of the clerk. We decided it would be necessary for us to find the actual handwriting of these persons.

In probate matters, that is, matters concerning wills and guardianships, the papers were handled differently. The original papers were retained in the clerk's office, not copied and returned like deeds. I decided to go to the archives in the courthouse of Harris County where old records are kept and see if I could find an original signature of either the man or his wife. I was delighted to find what I believed was a signature of Reuben. (The surname is omitted in this narrative.) I also discovered about that time in history, a certain man and his wife from this area died, leaving two minor children. Of course, a guardian had to be appointed by the county court to take care of the children and the property, which consisted of a herd of cattle. An application appeared for a man to be appointed guardian of these children. The Court acted upon it and appointed him guardian and, about two years after the appointment, I found in the records of that guardianship a paper that read something like this: We, the undersigned, friends and relatives of the two minor children, the subject of the above entitled guardianship, having their interest at heart, respectfully request the court to remove———— as their guardian and appoint in his stead, someone less ambitious for himself." This was signed by eight of the old ranchmen, many whose names are familiar to me yet. Included was the very beautiful, bold, plain handwriting of Reuben. I thought, "Now I have it. I can prove that Reuben could write." His handwriting was very good for that period of time. The paper was so old, it nearly fell to pieces, but I got a photostatic copy to introduce as evidence in that trial. I can almost see those old ranchmen riding from ranch to ranch with that paper to get signatures and saying to their neighbors, "He will steal those kids' cattle, and we've got to do something about it." Well, the court did remove him and appoint someone in his stead. But the interesting part of this story is that, when we got into trial, it was established beyond doubt that there were two couples that lived in the same period of time. One was a ranchman in Harris County and one was a ranchman in Chambers County. Two Reubens with the same surname had married Susans. The Reuben who had signed the statement in the guardianship was not the Reuben who had made his mark on the deed conveying Susan's interest in the land in controversy. We lost the case.

As I said, that went on in the courthouse I see two blocks from my window now. I remember something else I thought interesting and which I discovered in my studies in the Archives of the County Court House of Harris County, Texas. While looking for papers involving the estates of Reuben and Susan, I discovered a probate of a will of one of Susan's brothers whose name was Henry. He left a will which was probated in the Harris County Court prior to the Civil War. The probate code (then being similar to what it is now) provided that if a will was written and the maker of the will named no executor, then the will would stand and the Court would appoint what is called "Administrator with will annexed". When this becomes necessary, the Court will appoint the nearest of kin of the deceased as administrator.

Henry's will read something like this: "I leave all of the property I own at my death to Priscilla West, in appreciation of the kindness she showed me, and the care she took of me while I was wounded at the Garner Ranch in Orange County, Texas." (Incidentally, the Garner Ranch he spoke of was the ranch of my great-great grandfather, Bradley Garner, mentioned in a former chapter.) The Priscilla named in the will was the daughter of a neighboring ranchman. It is quite clear to me now that this man, Henry, while working cattle in Orange County, was injured by a horse or shot and Priscilla, the neighboring girl, nursed him back to health.

A long time after he made the will, he died and, in the meantime, Priscilla had married Phillip Tarkington, who settled where Tarkington's Prairie is now. Phillip, Priscilla's husband, filed the will for probate and Henry's brother contested it, claiming that Henry made the will, depending on Priscilla's promise to marry him, which she did not do. The court held that the will was good, the property belonged to Priscilla and that he had to appoint Henry's brother administrator as the law required. The administrator filed an inventory of Henry's property, which included, among other things, 85 head of cattle, 200 bundles of corn fodder, 1 negro slave (valued at $1,000) and a jug of whiskey (valued at $4.00). Incidentally, the cattle were valued at $5.00 a head.

According to the records, after the lapse of about one year, Phillip filed a request for the court to require the administrator to deliver the property to Priscilla. Thereupon the administrator filed a "corrected" inventory, stating that he was mistaken and that there were only 50 head of cattle, all of which he had to sell to pay Henry's debts. The record revealed that, after another year elapsed, Phillip filed another paper requesting the Court to require the administrator to deliver the negro slave to Priscilla. The administrator reported to the Court that the negro slave had escaped and gone to Matagorda County and could not be found. It appeared that Priscilla didn't get any of Henry's property after all. I imagine the administrator drank the jug of whiskey.

CHAPTER TWENTY-FIVE

WHO STOLE THE BOLIVAR CATTLE?

Galveston and its courthouse always brings to mind many stories including this one which involves some of my own family history and a man who, in the interest of propriety, I will call "John Smith". As stated in a former chapter, when we moved back to Hamshire in 1902, we brought our cattle to the Hamshire range since cattle raised on the lush salt grass near the coast will not winter well on the upper prairies. We would always herd our cattle back to Sabine Pass for the winter range and bring them back in the summer. That method kept the cattle fat, but it proved unprofitable in the end.

During one of the winters, while in my late teens, my father (who was in bad health and in need of cash) sent me to Sabine Pass to sell some steers. We did not sell calves in those days; cattle were not butchered for eating until they were old enough to have a good flavor. This generation sacrifices the real beef flavor for tenderness and does not know the taste of real good Texas beef. I took the train to Sabine Pass and got my father's first cousin, Cole McCall, to furnish a couple of cow ponies and help me gather fifteen fat three-year-old steers. I sold them, returned home and gave the money to Dad. He counted it, and said, "You got a good price, who did you sell them to?" I said, "John Smith. He was the only one buying cattle and is the only one in the butcher business at this time." Dad asked, "Did John go in the pasture and see the cattle?" I said "Yes" and Dad asked if there were any fat heifers in the pasture. I said that there were fifteen three-year-old heifers. He said, "They will not be there in the spring, when we go after the cattle." I really did not know the significance of this remark, but Dad walked out of the room, and my grandmother (his mother), who was visiting us at the time, said, "Well, John came by it honestly. You children should know that your grandfather, your father, and John's father were in the butcher business and your father quit because he didn't like the way the others were doing." I did not give it too much thought at the time, but when we went back to Sabine Pass in the spring for the cattle, the 15 fat heifers were gone and we never took our cattle back again.

This matter was brought to my mind many years later. After I established my law office in Beaumont, one of my clients happened to be an old man who had been foreman of one of the larger ranches at Sabine Pass in the early days and was familiar with the many things that went on there. He used to come to my office and talk about the old times. One day he said to me, "Do you know why your Pa quit the butcher business?" I said, "No, but my grandmother made some reference to it when I was a boy." He said "Well, he found out that his Pa and old man Smith were stealing cattle, and he would have no part of it." Since they were adept in the art of pickling beef and had a good market for it, I believe they would have done well if they had bought the cattle they butchered.

My grandfather's vocation has relevance to a case I once tried in Galveston. I was opposed in this trial by a very fine lawyer from Houston by the name of Homer Mabry and, while we were on opposite sides of this law suit, we were very good friends and carried on many interesting conversations during intervals in the trial. Homer was worried about a record title and, in trying to perfect his limitation title, tried to prove that the ancestors of his client, Shanghai Pierce, had fenced some land. While his witness was testifying, one of my clients whispered to me. "We know an old man who says that he built that fence." I said, "Get him here in the morning." I put the man on the stand the next morning. He was a very fine old man. He testified that he was eighty years of age and that he was born and lived his entire life on Bolivar Peninsula. I asked the question, "Mr. Hughes, do you remember anything about a fence that was built about sixty years ago across Bolivar Peninsula from the Gulf to the Bay? It was where Gilchrist is now." He said, "Yes, Pa and me built it." I said, "Then Shanghai Pierce never built it." He answered, "Oh, we never heard of Shanghai Pierce." I asked him why they built the fence. He answered, "Well, I'll tell you. We built it as a drift fence. There was no fence between Bolivar Point and Sabine Pass and, when mosquitoes would get bad and the wind would blow from the east, our cattle would drift all the way to Sabine Pass and we would never get them back." I said, "Thank you Mr. Hughes; no more questions."

There was a recess in the trial, and I said, "Homer, that thing nearly got out of hand." He said, "What do you mean? The old devil made a perfect witness." I said, "Yes, but did you notice how quickly I dropped it when he mentioned his cattle drifting to Sabine Pass? My grandfather was in the butcher business at that time and I know damn well that when Bolivar cattle drifted there, they would never come back."

CHAPTER TWENTY-SIX

LEADING QUESTIONS PAID OFF

I have never catered to criminal law. The part of my practice which I like is the law of real estate and the probate of estates. The practice of probate law brings mingled emotions of sorrow and pleasure. To me, criminal law does not have the fascination it has for some lawyers. Of course, it is gratifying to clear an innocent person accused of a crime, but what about the person you know is guilty? You have to take his case and you must try to clear him. I have said many times and I repeat, without fear of successful contradiction, that to be a successful criminal lawyer, from a pecuniary standpoint, you have to have some elements of a criminal.

I illustrate in this manner: a lawyer has a perfect legal and moral right to take the defense of a person accused of a crime, although he knows the client is guilty. The constitution of the State of Texas, as well as that of the United States, gives anyone accused of a crime the right to defense by a lawyer of his choice. When a lawyer takes the case, he has the duty, morally and legally, to defend the accused, to see that he gets a fair trial before a jury of his peers, and to see that he receives no more punishment than he deserves.

Now if a person indicted for a crime comes to employ me and I make a promise to see that he gets a fair trial and receives no more punishment than he deserves, he will say to me, "To hell with you. I do not want a fair trial. I do not want the punishment I deserve. I did what I have been indicted for". What he wants his lawyer to do is to produce evidence that does not exist.

I do not wish to imply that all criminal lawyers are criminal, but sometimes money does buy witnesses, resulting in a miscarriage of justice. A criminal goes free and somebody makes money out of it. It is very rare that a person indicted by a grand jury is not, to some extent, guilty of crime. Of course, there are instances where a prosecuting attorney is overly zealous to build a reputation and excessive punishment results. In such a case, the criminal lawyer has a great function to perform. I repeat that a grand jury very rarely indicts the wrong person and it is my opinion that the television shows you see, where the district attorney and other law enforcement officers are wrong, creates an unwholesome lack of respect in the minds of large segments of the population for law officers. These shows are very entertaining, but very unrealistic.

To illustrate how money and court room expertise can thwart justice, I will tell you of a lawyer I knew well, who had such a fine personality and knowledge of courtroom psychology that he could put on a better show in the courtroom, dealing in realities, than Perry Mason does on TV. Our friend seldom lost a criminal case and prospered financially, but it was often said of him that, when an indicted person sought his defense and the question of the amount of fee was discussed, his statement to the client would be, "That depends on whether you furnish the witnesses or expect me to do so." This man's shrewdness as a criminal lawyer is illustrated by the following true story.

I was not in the courtroom, but the story was related to me by persons who were. The incident occurred shortly after World War I. A certain young man was drafted, went through the entire war in Germany and returned uninjured physically. He left in the States his sweetheart to whom he was engaged and to whom he had sent all the money he had saved during the war. When he returned he found his sweetheart had another boy friend and all the money was gone. Perhaps because of the combination of his great disappointment and the psychological effect the war had on him, he waylaid his sweetheart and her boy friend and shot and killed both.

The family of the accused employed our friend, who was an outstanding criminal lawyer and, because of the newspaper publicity the affair had been given, he succeeded in getting a change of venue to another county in Texas where the incident was unknown. Our rules of evidence provide that a lawyer cannot ask his client on the witness stand a leading question; that is, a question so framed that the question suggests the answer. When such a question is asked, if the opposing counsel is alert, he will object to it before it is answered. It is the duty of the Court to sustain the objection and not permit the witness to answer the question.

Our friend, as is the custom, employed a young lawyer in the town where the trial was held to assist him in the case. There was a severance of the cases; the first trial was to be for the murder of the boy friend and the second

117

was for the murder of the sweetheart. The jury was selected and the trial began.

Our friend, knowing he had no defense, had to resort to other methods. The local district attorney presented his evidence and rested his case. Our friend put his client on the stand and began by asking him a very leading question. The district attorney objected, the judge sustained the objection and the defendant was not allowed to answer. Our friend then asked his client another leading question, to which the district attorney objected, the judge sustained the objection and the accused was not allowed to answer. At this point the judge said to our friend; "You must understand the rules of evidence better than you seem to; I warn you not to do that anymore." I can just see our dignified friend now, as he reared back and said, "I will try to refrain, Your Honor." He then directed to his client the most leading question he could frame. Again the district attorney objected, again the Court sustained the objection and the accused was not allowed to answer the question. The judge having become exasperated said to our friend: "If you persist in this, I shall have to fine you for contempt of court." Again, "I will try to refrain, Your Honor" and directed another question to his client as leading as he could frame it. The judge, whose patience was completely exhausted, said, "I fine you $50.00 for contempt of court."

In a dignified manner and in a voice for all the jury to hear, he replied: "I do not have $50.00, Your Honor." The judge replied, "You will have to go to jail." The young local lawyer, not having been told of the ruse, whispered to our friend, "I will lend you the $50.00." Our friend replied for the jury's hearing, "I will not accept charity." He then arose in his superb and dignified manner and said, "Gentlemen of the jury, I do not understand what is going on here. My client and myself are strangers in this town. He is on trial for his life and, for some reason we do not understand, the judge and the district attorney will not permit him to talk. I am going to jail now, and my young associate will close the case. Mr. Sheriff, I am ready." He then walked out of the courtroom with the sheriff. The jury, of course, knowing nothing of the rules of evidence, in their extreme sympathy gave the man three years suspended sentence for cold-blooded murder. This all happened so fast that the judge and the district attorney did not know what was happening to them. However, the client still had to be tried for the murder of the sweetheart. And, as this performance could not be repeated, the accused was sentenced to twenty years in the penitentiary.

The young man served his twenty years, returned to this area, began a new life and became a substantial citizen. Perhaps, because of the circumstances, this man did not deserve the death penalty for which the district attorney was asking, and our friend, in a very peculiar manner, performed a useful service.

The application of this rule against leading questions is further illustrated by the following story. To the layman it must be explained that appeals are taken from the District Court to the Courts of Appeal, of which there are eleven in Texas. On questions involving similar points of law, the lower courts are governed in their decisions by the holdings of the Courts of Appeal. Many years ago, the Chief Justice of the Amarillo Court of Appeals was a fine judge who handed down very good and very fair opinions. His personality was so constituted that it was difficult for him to keep comedy out of his court decisions, all of which are recorded in the Southwest Reporter.

There was a case tried in the District Court of a certain county and an appeal was taken to the Amarillo Court of Civil Appeals. As in criminal cases, when a lawyer asks a leading question in civil cases the opposing counsel should be alert and object before it is answered by the witness. Sometimes, however, the opposing counsel is so slow in reacting that the question is answered by the witness. In a situation like that, it is proper for the opposing counsel to ask the court to instruct the jury to disregard the answer. Sometimes a lawyer will tell his witness, when he is asked a certain question, to answer quickly. I am afraid I have been guilty of such conduct in the past.

In the case in question, the judge was confronted with a situation where, in the lower court, a question was answered before the opposing counsel objected. The opposing counsel finally got on his feet and asked the Court to instruct the jury to disregard the answer. This the Court refused to do, which was an error on the part of the trial judge and, on the basis of such refusal, the opposing counsel, who lost his case, appealed to the Court of Civil Appeals.

It came up for decision before our friend with a sense of humor. He was compelled to rule that the case had to be sent back for retrial because the trial judge was in error. He wrote, "The jury having heard the answer, the harm was done and the trial judge may have just as well thrown a polecat in the jury box and told the jury not to smell it." He was right. It has been my experience that, once a jury has heard the answer to a question, it is hard to erase it from their minds, and it is bound to affect their verdict.

CHAPTER TWENTY-SEVEN

TO WHOM DID THE COW BELONG?

I do not boast that I have won all of my cases. No lawyer who has tried many cases can truthfully say he has never lost a case. I do not even claim to have won a majority of my cases; I have kept no record. I hope, however, that I will be pardoned for having a more vivid memory of those I have won than those I have lost. I cannot help having a more vivid memory of those that had an element of human interest.

A good many years ago I was employed to assist a lawyer because of his belief I had some peculiar knowledge of a particular type of lawsuit. Whether he was right or wrong in his belief, we did win the case. I have often thought that this was one case won primarily on my argument to the jury. The facts are something like this: Our client, the defendant, was a woman who had a herd of Brahman cows in a pasture adjacent to the highway. She was negligent in maintaining her fences. Her husband had died some years before and left the cattle. Because she thought so much of them, she would not dispose of the cattle although she was unable to properly care for them and some often got out on the highway. It is strictly against the law to willingly permit cattle to run on the highway and, in a civil suit, if they are on the highway through your negligence and that negligence causes a wreck and an injury, you are liable in damages to the injured person.

On the night in question, two young men were driving a Lincoln along a wooded area of the highway adjacent to our client's pasture. One of the men was very seriously injured as a result of hitting a cow and he sued our client. While the plaintiff and his friend testified that they were only driving 55 miles an hour, which was the nighttime speed limit, other evidence showed that after hitting the cow in the middle of the road, the car immediately left the road, traveled along the rim of the road some 100 feet still carrying the cow, which the highway patrolman testified weighed 900 pounds, and side-swiped a large gum tree. At 200 feet, the car ran over and completely up-rooted a six-inch gum tree (still carrying the cow) and at 250 feet the car hit a 14-inch gum tree where the car went to pieces and the cow was tossed 70 feet beyond the point of impact. The driver of the car was severely injured but his companion was able to walk.

They both testified they were observing the speed limit. The driver was badly injured, and stated he had spent much time in the hospital. According to his testimony, he was lying on the road after the wreck in a semi-conscious condition before the ambulance arrived. The primary question was whether this cow belonged to the defendant. The uninjured companion testified that the driver had asked him before the ambulance arrived to see what brand was on the cow. He testified he did, and the brand was H F K. The highway patrolman who investigated the wreck said that he, using his flashlight, was unable to ascertain the brand. The jury had to determine what brand was on the cow. It became my duty to convince the jury that the young man was lying about his inspection of the brand.

Although this trial was twenty years ago, I think I can remember my argu-ment almost word for word. I like to talk to a jury. My experience as a juror many years before probably served me well. I had been on many juries and have, I believe, a good understanding of jury psychology. I said to them, "La-dies and gentlemen of the jury, the Court has asked you what the brand was on the cow that caused this wreck. The Court has told you that you are sole judges of the evidence and the credibility of the witnesses and the weight to be given their testimony. The companion of the injured man who has sued my client for $35,000, has testified that the injured man, while lying there waiting for the ambulance, asked him to examine the brand on the cow, which he said was H F K, in spite of the fact that the highway patrolman could not make it out. Now ladies and gentlemen, the Court expects you to call upon your experience in life in passing on the credibility of the witness and the weight to be given their testimony. Now you and I know that this young man, lying out there on the roadside, more dead than alive on that fa-tal night, was not thinking of building up evidence for a law suit against my client. He was thinking of home, family, God, dying and hoping that an am-bulance would soon come. Those cows in the pasture have been quite visible from the roadside ever since this occurred, and the remaining cattle bear a brand of H F K, which can readily be seen from the road. I believe your ex-perience in life will convince you that the highway patrolman was telling the

121

truth and that the brand was uninspected by this young man on that fatal night."

The jury was out five minutes and returned a verdict that it was not the defendant's cow. It has been twenty years since I tried that lawsuit, and I do not know yet to whom that cow belonged.

CHAPTER TWENTY-EIGHT

OUR LIBERAL HOMESTEAD LAWS

I think at this time it would be well to relate some facts that support my contention that our laws which exempt the homestead and other items of property from forced sale are too liberal. They favor the homestead claimant and are unfair to the person who has extended him credit. Nothing in our law has been more carefully guarded than the rights of minors, the rights of insane persons and the rights of persons to retain their homes and other property incident to a home against the claims of creditors.

Ever since statehood, there has been a law on the statutes that (except for taxes and the original purchase price) exempts a home owner from forced sale for debts. This exemption, so far as a rural homestead is concerned, can embrace two hundred acres (regardless of valuable improvements), all implements of husbandry, which now can be expensive farm machinery of unlimited value, five head of cows and their calves, food and forage for their livestock, food for home consumption, a cemetery lot and all tools of trade or profession. The statute, which has not been changed for 100 years, includes a team of horses, a wagon and a carriage. During the depression of the thirties when the banks had taken away all they could from the farmers, the legislature saw fit to add turkeys, geese, chickens, guineas, and the final irony of it all, one dog.

If a home is urban, the exemption extends to a lot or lots used for residence, provided the value of the lot did not exceed $10,000 at the time the homestead was acquired. The home on the lot, however, may be of unlimited value. The exemption may also protect a business of any location provided the combined value of the business and residential land did not exceed $10,000 when acquired and provided they are located in the same town.

I have put many farmers through bankruptcy where the creditors got very little, and the bankrupt client saved enough to start life over. I really believe our exemption laws are too liberal in favor of a home owner who has mortgaged his home, stating to the lender that he was not claiming it as his homestead, but later asserting that, at the time he made the loan, it was his home. I have been guilty in the past of taking advantage of those liberal sections of the law and am engaged in a law suit at this time where I am inclined to believe that the liberal construction in favor of the home owner will cost the client I represent $35,000.

The following story somewhat illustrates the working of our exemption laws in Texas. When the late Governor Ross Sterling was making his campaign for a second term, after having been a good Texas governor, he was involved in a bitter campaign for re-election against opponents who were abusing him. I was in an audience of about 2,000 people when he made a speech in a park in Port Arthur. He said he did not see how his opponent could have the gall to say such untrue things about him. "I believe," he said, "the gall is the biggest part about him. This brings to mind a story." As he stood on the speaker's rostrum that night, he went on to say that some years ago a man came into the black-land belt of Central Texas and bought a 200-acre farm, paying cash. He had plenty of money, built a fine home, furnished it with fine furniture, surrounded himself with fine farming tools and some livestock, acquired all food and forage necessary for home consumption, a fine automobile and a truck. But after running out of cash, he began to buy on credit in the little town. He owed the grocery, the drug store, the lumberman, the hardware store and also the bank. The depression of the early thirties struck, and the businessmen in the town were very hard pressed for money. Our farmer friend on the hill owed considerable money to them all. They discussed the matter in town and decided to go, as a committee, to the home of the farmer and try to persuade him to sell some of his property to pay them as much as he could. According to this story, he invited them into his living room and the spokesman told the story of their plight and asked that he sell part of his property and pay something on his debts.

He reared back in his easy chair and said: "Gentlemen, what you see here, all you see around you is exempt under the law to my family. I do not really own it. The only thing I own is my body, and if you want to cut that up and divide it among you, do so." The statement was so ridiculous that the whole committee was dumbfounded, except the old banker who was hard of hearing. Not having heard the statement, he leaned toward his nearest companion, and said "What did he say?" The companion told him. The old banker, after a slight hesitation said, "Well, I am the biggest creditor, ain't I?" Someone said, "Yes." The banker said, "When you cut him up, I want the gall, because that is the biggest part about him."

Another illustration of the liberal interpretation given by courts of the exemption law is a decision made by an appellate judge. The case involved a situation during the depression when a bank, to whom a central Texas farm owner owed a lot of money, had undertaken to sell five heifers to satisfy the debt to the bank. The farmer's lawyer went to trial court and asked the court to grant an injunction forbidding the bank to sell the heifers, based on the theory that they were exempt as a part of his homestead under the exemption law of the State of Texas. The Court ruled with the farmer and the bank appealed the case to the appellate court. The appellate judge recited the facts of the case in the trial court and then wrote, "Under the exemption law, one of the exemptions to the farmer is five milk cows and their calves. I do not see how a heifer which has had no relationship with a bull can be classified as a milk cow. We are supposed to follow precedent, that is the decisions handed down by our predecessors in these courts and, since one of my honorable predecessors has seen fit to look upon a truck and call it a wagon, and another of my predecessors has seen fit to look upon a Ford car and call it a carriage, and even another has seen fit to look upon a mule, son of a jackass, and call it a horse, I therefore feel constrained and it is my duty, to look upon a heifer and call it a milk cow." It was so held that the heifers were exempt from forced sale.

This exemption is a part of the constitution of Texas and, when adopted about a hundred years ago, a lot of farm land was worth no more than three dollars per acre; whereas now, a 200-acre farm with improvements, may be worth $200,000. It can be seen that a farmer may be rich and not required to pay his debts. Last year a constitutional amendment was submitted to the voters of Texas which would reduce the rural homestead exemption to 50 acres. This amendment was overwhelmingly defeated.

Texas seems to be the best place in the world to beat your creditors. Another exemption is current wages for personal services. Such are not subject to garnishment in the hands of the employer. I know many men who are making $1200 a month in wages and no part of it can be touched by creditors, even a family doctor or the groceryman.

CHAPTER TWENTY-NINE

LIBERAL DIVORCE LAWS OR TRIAL MARRIAGES

I have tried to show the economic changes in the last three quarters of this century. Since my experience in life has enabled me to gain a peculiar knowledge of the vicissitudes of domestic relations and, in view of the fact there is a lot of concern over the increasing divorce rate and the alleged breaking down of morals since the passing of the Victorian Age, I thought it well to make some comment on the matter.

Ever since the author of Genesis quoted God as saying "It is not good for man to live alone," importance of the man and woman relationship has been realized. I am sure that His statement was not meant from the standpoint of procreation alone.

Woman is the greatest gift of God to man, but unfortunately, he has too often failed to understand the obligation which accompanies the gift. No artist has ever painted a picture equal to the love-light in a woman's eyes beheld by a man who has kindled that light. On the other hand, nothing is more depressing than the expression on a woman's face who has been neglected, abused or spurned.

I don't mean to imply that all domestic upheavals are to be blamed on men; I have seen both sides of the picture many times. I think it is safe to say that I have, during my 43 years of practice, obtained 1000 divorces. These have ranged all the way from two couples going before the court and the defendant admitting to the plaintiff's grounds and the parties parting friends, to cases involving the division of over half a million dollars worth of property and the custody of children. I have one case in mind that required six years for final disposition. Different phases of the case went to the court of civil appeals twice and finally back to the court of domestic relations where it was finally resolved.

Until 1971, the Texas law recognized only five grounds for divorce, one of which was cruelty. The statute provided that a party was entitled to a divorce if the other party had been guilty of such harsh, cruel and tyrannical treatment of such a nature as to render living together as husband and wife insupportable. It would appear that the word, "insupportable" is not widely used elsewhere in the English language and it took several years for the courts to define what the legislature meant. Of course, it was the duty of a judge to deny the divorce unless the facts met the definition. I think it is safe to say that three-fourths of the divorces which I handled were obtained on the ground of cruelty. I further confess that many, many times the facts did not meet the court's definition of the statute. Under such circumstances, it was the duty of the judge to deny the divorce.

I only remember one occasion where I was chased out of the courthouse because sufficient facts were not proven to justify the granting of a divorce. In that instance, my client lied to me about the alleged cruel acts of his wife. When the case was tried he could prove no cruel treatment. It has always been my custom when a person comes to me for a divorce to explain the law and the facts which must exist to entitle the plaintiff to a divorce. I said to them, "I do not know the facts, but they must meet the law and, if the case is not contested, only God and the judge will know what you told him."

To illustrate the point, I'll relate an instance which happened before a fine old judge who was religiously inclined and a strict interpreter of the law. Several other lawyers and myself were in the court trying a land case. There was a lull in the proceedings. While a plaintiff was having his secretary dictate the charge to the jury, a very young lawyer walked in with a young client and asked the judge if he had time to hear an uncontested divorce. The judge said to bring the client in. The young lawyer brought the client before the judge's bench and made the preliminary proof which, at that time, required the plaintiff be a resident of the State of Texas for a year and of the county for six months. The young lawyer said to his client, "You sued your wife for divorce alleging cruelty; what did she do?"

"She slapped me", was his reply. There was a pause and the lawyer asked no more questions.

The judge looked up and said, "Is that all she did?" The client answered, "Yes, sir."

"She slapped you just one time?"

"Yes, sir."

"Well, you can't get any divorce in my court on those grounds." The young lawyer started to protest and the judge said, "No, no, no, you have proved no grounds for a divorce."

Some judges would have granted a divorce, but this old judge was entirely right, because the courts had held many times that every little friction, every little argument with minor abuse did not meet the definition of making their living together insupportable. We felt sorry for the young lawyer but the judge actually shooed him out of the courtroom.

My opponent in the case we were trying was a very fine old lawyer, a life-long friend of the judge. We sat there listening to this proceeding and finally, when the papers came back he rose to his feet and said, "Your Honor, I'm ready now to produce my motion in this case that has been prepared, but before I do, I want to appear before this court as "amicus curiae". This term means, "a friend of the court" and, if a judge is in error, any member of the bar has a right to point it out to him. Obviously, however, it is seldom done.

The old judge looked at the lawyer as if to say, "What are you going to tell me about the law?" The old lawyer said, "Your Honor, we as lawyers and as husbands of this community want to protest against the ruling in that divorce case. If our wives can slap us around promiscuously and we can't do anything about it, we want to file our protest."

The old judge saw that it was a joke and he said, "Ike, you know that man didn't prove grounds for divorce. I say that women, since they have asserted the right to cuss, drink and smoke, may have a right to one slap." As a matter of law, the old judge was correct.

There was another incident that occurred in my own practice. I was hired by a woman who had been sued by her husband and, while she was very distressed and did not want the divorce, there were some property rights involved. She asked me to appear at the trial in her behalf and see that her property rights were protected. At that time there was another fine judge of the domestic relations court in our county. He always held his divorce cases around the table in the courtroom and not from his bench. We all gathered around the table and the plaintiff's lawyer made the preliminary proof of residence and venue and then he said to his client, "You have sued your wife for divorce. What did she do?" "Oh nothing, I would come home drunk once in a while." The lawyer was very much surprised by his client's answer and said nothing. The old judge looked up and said to the client, "How often does this happen?"

"Oh, every two or three weeks."

"And what would she do when you came home drunk and raising hell?"

"Oh, nothing."

The old judge said, "Well you can't get any divorce in my court. Now if your wife wants a divorce she can get it but you can't."

I felt very sorry for the lawyer who was a good friend of mine and, as we walked out of the courtroom, I said to him, "Possibly, my client who is not here, will permit me to file a cross action in this case. If she does, we'll dispose of this matter." I consulted and she said she was willing to get the divorce on a cross action if the properties were properly cared for. I filed the cross action and in due course of time, I brought her before the judge. I explained to him that this was the cross action of the case he had denied a few weeks before. He said, "Lady, I've heard the evidence, divorce granted." The point is, the complaining party needed grounds for divorce or a reason why it should be granted under the law.

The law has now been changed and much criticism has been directed at the change. It provides a divorce can be granted through no fault of either party if there is conflict of personalities which cannot be resolved and which renders their living together as husband and wife insupportable. In my view, I must come to the defense of the legislature for making that change. The only sad part is if there are minor children. The legislature has gone all out to see they are properly protected with respect to material matters and that they have companionship of both parents if both are worthy.

Our Victorian parents would have raised their eyebrows in astonishment if anyone had suggested trial marriages, but when the situation is properly analyzed, that is exactly what we have. Two persons can marry, find that they have a conflict of personalities and one files for a divorce. The case has to be filed sixty days before it can be granted and, after the divorce is granted, there is a prohibition against remarriage for another 30 days. So, if a person is financially able to do so, he can easily make two tries in marriage in one year.

I have never seen the court deny a divorce since the law has been changed, basing the grounds strictly on a conflict of personalities. I do not know exactly how the courts define "the conflict of personality" but they have so far been very liberal. I recall an instance when I represented the defendant. The lawyer for the plaintiff was asking questions of his client. The law was new and he did not know exactly what he had to prove to show a conflict. He was not getting very far with it so I said, "Judge, can't you see that one of these parties has brown eyes and the other has blue eyes? Isn't that a conflict of personalities?" He said, "I guess so," and he granted the divorce.

The smart ones are those who settle these matters amicably. Nothing creates more animosity and has so much bad effect on children as a court battle over a divorce. When people find in later life that they have made a mistake and they are living in misery, why shouldn't they go their separate ways and start a new life for themselves? I've seen some very happy results in such situations.

I do not claim to have a solution for these domestic relation problems. I've seen some teenage marriages turn out all right, but I've seen many, many others that did not. But where will you place the blame? Thousands of youngsters, when making the decision to become man and wife, are in such an emotional upheaval that they are wholly unfit to enter into the most important contract of their lives. And why condemn a law that would sanction the correction of a youthful mistake and allow the parties to start a new life when they are more mature and more emotionally stable? I've been contacted by many women in their thirties or forties, often in tears, who were confronted with the necessity of a divorce. I say to them, "Why not make a new life for yourself. You're now old enough to make some man a good wife. You now know that teenage arrangement was an error."

On the other hand I have talked myself out of many a divorce fee when I realized, after consultation, that the domestic upheaval of the parties was based entirely upon unfounded suspicion or petty intolerances or selfishness which should be overcome by the parties assuming a proper attitude toward the marriage relationship. A relationship between a man and a woman should never be consummated by marriage unless the greatest motive of each party is the happiness of the other. Too often the motive is the selfish desire to dominate another person's life. It has been wisely said that many marriages have broken up very fine friendships. Frequently one party or the other feels the relationship is a sort of slavery. There is too often a feeling that "You're married to me now, so I will tell you what you can and cannot do."

Quite often domestic upheavals leading to divorce start with some wholly unfounded suspicion. If a husband leaves his work or office and decides to spend some time with some friends over a cup of coffee or a bottle of beer and is a few minutes late, his wife is bound to believe he has been out with his secretary. She should meet him with a kiss and a hearty welcome even though he is a little late and not question where he has been. No one likes to be checked on and her questioning and nagging is bound to lead to bad results. The same is true when a wife returns from her hairdresser a little late. The questions, "Where have you been? Why are you so late?", are bound to start trouble. Such little instances have often led to the courthouse. Even if the husband in the instance mentioned above had been out with his secretary, if the wife greets him cheerfully with a kiss, he may soon forget the secretary and realize that what he has at home is something far better, lasting and substantial than a frivolous flirtation.

There is another thing I often tell young married people. The first thing you should do is build a home and make it so comfortable and so attractive that you would rather be there than any place in the world. And to married people, I'd say to both the husband and wife, "Keep yourself so attractive that the original attraction that drew you together will continue." Too often the young husband comes to breakfast unshaven and ungroomed with a newspaper and a cup of coffee trying to overcome a hangover from the night before. And the wife immediately thinks, "Oh, my God, is this what I have married." I would say to young married people: keep yourself attractive, even more so than during courtship and there would be fewer divorces. I once represented a Madam of a house of prostitution and I think her philosophy was good. She said, "You know, if wives took more care of their appearance after marriage, we girls would starve to death."

So-called sex education that we hear so much about today is probably all right; I'll not comment on that. But that is not enough preparation for marriage; young people should be taught the temperamental qualities and shortcomings of the opposite sex. Too many men fail to recognize that a woman is a creature who must be made to know by acts and words that she is loved and appreciated. She not only needs a present feeling of security but a sense of continued security. No matter if her closets are overflowing with wearing apparel, she needs something new and pretty occasionally. And no matter how short money may be, a wife's visit to the hairdresser occasionally is the best investment a man can make. Men are so constituted that they need their ego stimulated constantly. And if the wife does not look after that matter, some other woman may.

Marriage is the greatest partnership in the world and it should last for a lifetime, but it takes two intelligent, tolerant and unselfish people to make a success of it. It often fails because the partners fail to know, or they have never been taught, the temperamental dispositions of the other sex. Perhaps I've said earlier in this chapter that I feel somewhat qualified to give advice along these lines because of my broad legal experience in such matters. I do not know whether this advice will be taken, but I hope I will be forgiven by other members of my profession if, to some remote degree, I prevent divorces which have become a very lucrative part of the practice of some lawyers.

CHAPTER THIRTY

MAMA, CAN I SAY "HELL" TO THAT MAN?

I am reminded of another case I tried about thirty-five years ago which illustrates the rule of evidence and the fact that a child was well raised. The father of the child came to my office and engaged me to file suit against the Santa Fe Railroad. The facts he related to me were true except that he exaggerated the injury of the child.

The facts he gave me were something like this: These people lived in a small town called Pineland, Texas. The child was five years of age. The grandmother decided to visit some people in Louisiana and took the child with her. They boarded the train and the grandmother went to sleep. There was another woman with a child about the same age on the train and the two children started playing in the aisle of the coach. Pujo, Louisiana, was not a town, but merely a flag stop for the train. There was no depot, depot agent, or anyone at the station; it was in the middle of the piney woods, a veritable wilderness. The other lady and her child got off at Pujo and were met by an automobile which carried them away. The colored brakeman, whose duty it was to assist people from the train, helped the lady off, her little girl, and also the little girl in question. The result was that the little child was left alone on the tracks in the middle of the wilderness and, of course, in her fright, began running down the track to catch the train.

After the train had gone several miles, the grandmother awoke and, missing the child, gave an alarm. The trainmen started moving the train back, believing the child had fallen off. They met her about a quarter of a mile from the place she had gotten off, running down the track, trying to catch the train, sustaining no physical injuries other than a few briar scratches.

132

The case was set for trial on a certain Monday morning in the District Court in Beaumont and, as was my custom before trying a case, I went to view the scene of the happening. I went by auto with the father to the station at Pujo, made an examination of the surrounding conditions and then went on to the home of my client where I had supper. Before supper, I called the little girl to me, told her who I was, and asked her if she would be able and willing to go down to Beaumont and tell several men in the courtroom what happened that day. This was two years after the incident and the little girl was then 7 years of age. She said she could and she related the happenings in a very vivid manner. She said, "I was playing with the little girl and the black conductor helped the little girl off, and helped me off, and they left, the train left, and I was scared, and I ran down the railroad track trying to catch the train." It was a very clear story of what happened.

To make my point, a child is permitted to testify as a witness provided the child, upon questioning by the judge or the attorney, demonstrates that it knows the meaning of the oath and understands the consequence of false swearing. In order to prepare her for the questions which she would be asked in the courtroom, I said: "Little girl, do you know what it means to take an oath, and tell the truth?" "Yes," she said, "It means you swear to tell the truth." "Now do you know what happens to little girls who do not tell the truth?" She hung her head and did not answer. About that time her grandmother called us to supper. I said to her, "Think about it, I will talk to you some more after supper." We had not much more than sat down when her mother came in laughing, and said that the child had called her off and said, "Mama, would it be all right if I said 'Hell' to that man?" Of course, that was just the answer I wanted. It showed that she understood that there was some kind of punishment for false swearing.

The next morning, when we tried the case, she made a perfect witness in every respect. Although only seven years of age, I have often thought she was the smartest person in the courtroom. Her demeanor was such that any thought the incident had adversely affected her mind or interrupted her scholastic development was completely dispelled. However, the jury gave her $500.00 for her fright and the few berry-vine scratches she received.

CHAPTER THIRTY-ONE

THE LAND TITLE THAT CHECKED BACK TO GOD

While every phase of the law has its attraction for me, I think the laws pertaining to real estate are the most fascinating. Does not everything that makes for human welfare come from the land or the sea? Isn't it true that all food must come from the land or the sea, either directly or indirectly? From the same sources come all products made of any kind of metal as well as clothing of every kind. Energy, which is so important, came first from the trees that grew in the soil, then coal which was mined from the land and then petroleum and gas.

Man is not free from greed. There have been disputes over land since the strife between the herdsmen of Lot and Abraham until the present time, and such disputes will continue until the end of the history of mankind. These disputes may be between a landlord and tenant as to whom is entitled to possession of a house or an apartment, or it may involve a boundary-line dispute over land that was once too cheap to justify a survey and now has become valuable oil or mineral-producing land. Disputes may arise over land that was once cheap farming or grazing land and has become valuable urban property.

I have in mind several 20-acre tracts of land within five miles of my home which sold for $3.00 per acre in 1895 and which I sold in 1925, while in the land business, for $50.00 per acre. Later oil was discovered and they have each produced over $1,000,000 worth of oil. Of course, such occurrences cause any flaw in the title to be found and corrected. An owner of land may be very honest and yet have flaws in his land title of which he has no knowledge if he is not familiar with land law. His land title may be adversely affected by marriage, divorce, death, birth, judgements, income tax or other taxes he has failed to pay. A lawyer representing a purchaser of valuable land has a great responsibility. Persons buying land should be represented by a competent lawyer or require a policy of title insurance. You cannot afford to buy land as you buy groceries.

I do not know the origin of the following story or whether it is true, but it does illustrate the point. There was a man of some means who traveled from New York to New Orleans. While there he found some real estate he thought would be a good investment. Being a very careful man, before he made the investment he wrote his New York lawyer a letter which read as follows: "Dear John, I am in New Orleans and have found some real estate which I think will be a good investment. However, I do not trust these Frenchmen down here. I have made them furnish me an abstract of the title of the land which goes all the way back to the U. S. Government, which purports to show every transaction with reference to the land, from the original purchaser from the government to the present owner. I want you to examine this title from the abstract which I am sending. Do not stop there. I want you to go back as far as possible into this title, because, as I have said above, I do not trust these people."

John, the lawyer in New York, seeing that his client was unduly disturbed, and seeing some comedy in the situation, kept the abstract for about a month and then wrote his client as follows: "Dear Bill, I have received the abstract covering the property which you plan to buy. The abstract shows a perfect claim of title from the U. S. Government to the present owner, the person from whom you propose to buy; but, noting the concern as expressed in your letter and your instructions to go back as far as possible, I thought it my duty to see if the U. S. Government really owned the land. I studied some American history and learned that Napoleon had won the Louisiana Territory by war and conquest from Spain. How did Spain get it? Now a further study of history revealed to me that Spain acquired it by discovery by Christopher Columbus. Now here I ran into a problem. Did Columbus have any right to make that voyage of discovery? Then a study of Spanish history revealed that the Queen of Spain authorized him to make the voyage. Did she have any right to authorize the voyage? A further study revealed that she consulted the Pope in Rome. Now by what authority did the Pope have the right to permit the voyage? Since it has not been successfully disputed that the Pope is the earthly representative of Jesus Christ and that Jesus is the Son of God, I advise you that you will have a good title."

CHAPTER THIRTY-TWO

A CASE WON BY THE DICTIONARY

There are many methods used in the trial of a lawsuit, whether civil or criminal, to persuade the court that your theory of the case is the correct one. What makes the work so laborious is there are seldom two sets of facts exactly alike. A lot of reading of decisions of the appellate courts are required in order to find what we lawyers call a "case in point". We often have to go into court with briefs prepared after much reading of the decisions of appellate courts. Frequently we carry books into the courtroom to read court decisions in an attempt to convince a court that the cases we have to support our contentions pertain to the facts at hand. I do not believe, however, that I ever won a case strictly on the dictionary rather than on law books, except in the incident related below.

My client was a large rice farmer and adjoining his land was a large ranch, entirely fenced in. There was a dry summer, the grass in the pasture was dead and the rice field, being well irrigated, attracted the cattle to the lush rice and water. The rice farmer, my client, finding it impossible to keep the cattle from breaking through the fence at night, employed a hand to go into this pasture and drive the cattle several miles into the pasture so they would not get back to the rice field before morning and destroy his rice during the night.

When the ranchman found this out, he was greatly displeased because the cattle, being driven several miles a day, were reducing their flesh to where they were not doing well. An argument arose and, although my client was warned, he persisted in having his man make those evening drives. The ranchman went to the district attorney who found a criminal statute written by the legislature in the early 1870's when trail drives were going through Texas to the Kansas railroad. When a trail drive was passing through an open-range territory, other cattle would join a herd and would be carelessly left in the herd. Having no particular intention to steal, when they got to Kansas, the trail drivers sold the cattle with their herd. The statute provided that it was an offense to drive cattle from their accustomed range.

Usually, when we have a case where a statute is involved, we check to see if there has ever been a court decision interpreting the statute. I examined and found none. My client was terribly worried; he was sure he was going to jail for a long time. The ranchman was a good friend of the county attorney and they were really after him. Not being able to find a court decision interpreting the statute and being desperate to prove my point, I began to wonder about the meaning of the word "range". Some months before that, at an unguarded moment, a salesman had talked me into purchasing a large dictionary of two volumes. To be rid of him, I signed the agreement and some weeks later, when the books came C. O. D., I angrily paid the delivery man and tossed them in the corner of my office unopened. To determine the exact meaning of "range", I decided to open the package. This was a standard dictionary and the compiler would often give a definition and quote from some standard work to illustrate. When I turned to the word "range," it said "an open area where cattle grazed, as distinguished from a pasture." And, to prove the point, the author of the dictionary quoted a paragraph from *The Virginian,* by Owen Wister.

I went to the courthouse armed with nothing more than the dictionary. The morning was absorbed in jury selection and the judge told us to be back at 1:30 to start the trial. I met the district attorney at lunch and I said to him, "Tom, how do you expect to win that case?" He said, "Why easy, that man is driving those cattle from their accustomed range every night, and driving all the fat off of them." I said, "Tom, do you know the definition of the word, 'range'?" He said, "I think so."

"Well, look at this definition."

He read it, went back and dismissed the case.

CHAPTER THIRTY-THREE

CROSS-EXAMINATION — THE SMOKING PISTOL

The following story is not original. I do not believe it is contained in any book; therefore, I cannot quote the author. However, it does illustrate some methods lawyers use in the trials of lawsuits.

I have stated previously that leading questions to your own witness are prohibited, but when you have a witness on cross-examination (that is the witness that the other party has called) you are unlimited in what you may ask him. Sometimes we lawyers get too enthusiastic and go too far. This story illustrates the fact that, when the witness has answered a question that establishes your point, you had better quit right then because, if you start badgering him, he may get you into trouble.

The story goes like this. A man was driving a horse and buggy on a narrow mountain ledge. There was no room for vehicles to pass. Another man approached him from the rear in an automobile and, being impatient and wanting the man and buggy to get out of the way, he began sounding his horn, making a great deal of noise. The horse, not being accustomed to automobiles, became frightened, reared up and fell over the cliff with buggy, man and all. The horse had a broken leg, the buggy was demolished and the man had many severe injuries including a broken leg, a broken shoulder, a broken collar bone and several broken ribs. He sued the driver of the automobile. When his lawyer placed him on the stand, he described the incident, telling what happened and describing his condition. He was still in a cast.

The defense lawyer took him on cross-examination and said to him, "Now you have told this court and this jury that you received these injuries from that accident. Isn't it true that, immediately after the accident, the man driving the automobile, my client, came back and asked you if you were all right and you said, 'Yes, I'm all right'?" The witness said, "Yes, I told him I was all right."

The defense attorney should have let it go and stopped there, but he also asked, "Now, how do you justify the conflict in your testimony?" The witness responded, "Well, sir, I'll tell you. It happened just like I told it. I was driving my horse and buggy down the narrow ledge and the man came up behind me blowing his horn. This scared my horse, he reared up and the horse, buggy and myself all went down the ledge. The horse's leg was broken, the buggy was demolished and I was injured as I just described. Yes, the man did get out of the car and walk back to the horse and, seeing the horse had a broken leg, he pulled out his pistol and shot the horse. He then walked over to me and said, 'Are you all right?' I answered, 'Yes, I am all right.' You see, he was still holding the smoking pistol!"

CHAPTER THIRTY-FOUR

RACE RELATIONSHIPS

Since I decided to name this book "The Memoirs and Philosophy of a Country Lawyer", a prospective reader who picks it up may expect it to contain more than the history of my life and an account of the cases which I have won and lost. The reader may find the name wholly inappropriate, but Webster defines philosophy as a search for the truth through logical reasoning.

I feel sure that a person who has lived through more than three quarters of a century and whose work and other experiences in life have thrown him in contact with every kind of person, regardless of race, creed, color, sex and environmental background, cannot have failed to form some ideas and take the proper philosophical approach to many situations.

The whites and blacks have been thrown together in a common society through no fault of anyone in the last three generations. To make things work as they should in a proper society both whites and blacks will have to live down their prejudices and complexes. I would say without fear of contradiction that both superiority and inferiority complexes exist and their existence intensifies the problem. I am well aware that many injustices occurred in what is known as the "deep south". These injustices were not caused solely by such complexes but were caused largely by political errors.

In the part of Texas where I was raised, the post-Civil War problem was not great. Slave ownership in our community was not a special way of life. A ranchman may have had one or two slaves which he brought from the southern states but the rigors of pioneer life and the interdependence between master and slave for survival resulted in mutual respect and admiration. I know such feelings existed during my lifetime, the second and third generation after the Civil War.

The children and grandchildren of former slaves were good people on the whole. The men made excellent cowhands and the women were excellent cooks and what are now called "babysitters". But there was mutual respect and every person was respected for the part he played in society. During my young manhood I hired many black men on the farm. I had sympathy and respect for their place in society and never believed they were entitled to abuse. I worked side by side with them and never let one do more of the hard work than I. As I write this, my mind recalls Jack Pilat. Jack was a powerful young black man about 24 years of age, weighing about 180 lbs. He was about my age and weight when he worked for me during the years 1915 and 1916. Our attitude toward our work and toward each other is probably illustrated best by an incident which occurred one hot July day when Jack and I were splitting cypress fence posts in the woods. We were both stripped to our waists and sweating profusely. I sawed a post-length piece off a large cypress log and was ready to use the axe-wedges and malls in splitting it into posts. I looked down at the log and said, "Jack, this is going to be a tough one." Without a second's hesitation Jack retorted, "Dat's all right, white folk, we'll just get tough with it."

I think my relationship with this man and others pretty well illustrates the relationship generally between white employers and black employees of those times. Yes, we ate at different tables, lived in different houses and attended different schools and churches. Does anyone expect the social customs in a society to change immediately without strife after generations of master and servant relationships?

The lawmakers were right to wait until the third generation after freedom to pass integration laws. Equal civil rights are always proper but social changes must be brought about by social evolution with perhaps a boost now and then to off-set outgrown prejudices. Everyday we see evidence of how the black man has taken his place in the political and economic life of the country, a place to which he has a God-given right if he earns it. The fact that he has attained this position, despite his heritage, should abolish such inferiority complexes that exist because of black skin. I have no patience for the white or black who takes the position that the blacks should be compensated for his underprivileged years and the fact that his ancestors came as slaves. Slavery was a fact of history, which, within very few generations brought the black man from barbarism to a place in a free society. With few exceptions, this freedom was attained without his firing a shot in the battle for it; perhaps few people in history attained such liberties as easily. Let the white man contemplate the imperfections of his own race and look with favor upon the accomplishments of the black who had a more unfortunate background. Let him drop his superiority complex, so that the races may live together in harmony. Some shudder to think of the possibilities of race amalgamation, but if it comes within the next few centuries and color lines are erased through biological evolution, so be it.

CHAPTER THIRTY-FIVE

IT IS NOT THE HIGH COST OF LIVING,
BUT THE COST OF HIGH LIVING

This is being written in 1976. I hear so much bunk and political propaganda with reference to the high cost of living and unemployment that I feel constrained to correct it. We may have the cost of high living now, but we certainly do not have the high cost of living. We are living in economic luxury compared to the situation that existed when I worked for a dollar a day 65 years ago. I was working on farms with the grandparents of clients I now have. We were getting one dollar a day and glad of it. That one dollar was not for eight hours of easy work; that was from sun to sun in hard manual labor.

I do not know when this will be read, if at all, but I am speaking of living costs in the first decade of this century as compared with 1976. Yard men and the very cheapest farm labor now receive $20.00 per day for 8 hours. I am talking about thoroughly unskilled labor. In this area, southeast Texas, everybody that wants work is working, and very few unskilled persons are working for less than $20.00 a day. They are not available because a boy with no education can go into the oilfield, the refineries, on pipelines or construction work and make a minimum of $32.00 a day. Very common unskilled laborers with no experience at all, for whom we are begging, can't be found. There is no unemployment in this area.

It is interesting to compare our living standard in 1907 with that of one earning only $20.00 today. If we take $2.00 of that $20.00 and give it to Uncle Sam, who then gives it to the unemployed, that leaves us $18.00 a day for 8 hours. When we were getting $1.00, it's true, we could go to the grocery store and buy a dozen eggs for 10 cents. They were kept in a basket after being bought from farmers perhaps two weeks before. We purchased them and took them home. Of course, we could not fry them; we had to scramble them if they did not smell too bad, which they often did. The grandchildren of my former co-employees have about $18.00 left from their day's work compared to $1.00 I had. Eighteen times the 10 cents I paid for the eggs, would amount to $1.80. Yesterday, I bought a dozen nice fresh, well kept eggs, which will fry "straight up" for 70 cents — not $1.80. We could buy flour at $1.00 for a 48 pound bag. Of course, my mother often had to sift it to get the weevils out and sometimes, when they got too numerous, she would have to throw a large portion of the sack away. I bought flour yesterday, not at eighteen times that price, but ten times that price. It was packed in a nice package and there is absolutely no loss; it doesn't even have to be sifted. We could go to the grocery store in those days with that dollar I earned for a day of labor and buy beef steak at 15¢ a pound. I bought beef yesterday, not eighteen times 15¢ (which would be $2.70 a pound) but at $1.50 per pound. This was not beef that was kept in a market where flies buzzed around and a part of which would have to be thrown away when I got home, but it was beef steak well wrapped in a sanitary cellophane bag with no loss. At the grocery store where I went as a boy, we could buy bacon at 15¢ a pound. This bacon was packed in big boxes and shipped in. Sometimes when we went to use it, it was rancid and had to be thrown away. Yesterday I bought bacon at $1.20, not eighteen times 15¢ (which would be $2.70). It was well wrapped in a cellophane package, clearly sanitary, ready for cooking with no loss. And on down the line, everything was about twice as high as it is now compared to the earning power of the common laborer. Coffee was bought cheap. Sure, it was green coffee; it had to be parched and ground. But the prepared coffee you buy today does not cost half what it cost us then, when compared with relative earning power.

The housewife now does her shopping in a nice, pleasant, air-conditioned supermarket where everything is well labeled and well prepared. She can buy food for half of what it cost my mother. Housewives today drive to the supermarket in an air-conditioned car. If my mother could not get some of the men folk, she would have to hitch up a horse and buggy and drive to market regardless of the weather or number of mosquitoes.

In reference to automobiles, during the time when the laborers were getting $1.00 a day, I bought a brand new automobile for $500.00. It was a T-model Ford, no windows, no self-starter and no air-conditioning. They had rubber tires on them but, if one drove the 20 miles to Beaumont and back without a flat, he was lucky. Such a car, well cared for, would perhaps travel

20,000 miles before it went to pieces. Two years ago I bought a brand new Cadillac for 15 times $500.00 with every modern convenience: power steering, air-conditioning, power brakes, power windows and radio. I have driven it two years without any trouble.

What I have said about groceries is true about clothing, houses and everything else that a person buys. The grandchildren of my former co-employees, even those who have acquired no skills whatsoever, are living in brick homes and driving the best automobiles. One seldom sees an old dilapidated car on the road anymore. Almost everyone has color television, never works more than 8 hours a day and has lots of time to spend in beer joints and watching T.V. I get thoroughly disgusted with the gripe about the high cost of living and the political promises of the politicians who are seeking offices. I still say the good old days were not the first decade of this century, but right now, and we haven't got sense enough to appreciate it. The point I am making is that now in 1976, Americans earning minimum wages are getting twice as much of the necessities and luxuries of life, at present earnings for 8 hours of easy work, as we got in 1907 for 12 hours of hard manual labor.

CHAPTER THIRTY-SIX

TRIBUTE TO WOMANHOOD

As a tribute to my wife who was my support and inspiration during the hard years and the years that followed, and as a tribute to many other wonderful women I have known, I feel this further comment appropriate. I am inclined to believe that an account of the events over the past three-quarters of a century would not be proper or complete without showing the change in the relationship of men and women to each other and to society as a whole. In addition, I include my prophecy of the future role of women.

Having professionally and otherwise been thrown into contact with every type of women and men, I make this statement expecting contradiction. Women as a whole, giving the word "character" its proper definition, have more character than men. It is true that God, in his plan for the perpetuation of the species, gave women a certain weakness, but with the responsibility of motherhood, she was given a strong moral quality. This attribute has and will make itself manifest more and more in the business and political life of mankind.

I have no patience with the present women's liberation movement. I do not believe that in this field or any other field, social changes should be accelerated by law. Changes will take place naturally in the evolutionary process.

Since medical science and changes in moral and religious concepts have made childbearing a privilege and not a burden, and other scientific developments have taken away many of the burdens of homemaking, women will take their place more and more in business and the political life of the community. In the business world women are now indispensable. In our practice and business we have five women who are superb in their work and, in our situation and in many other offices with which I am familiar, the work would be intolerable without them. I cannot conceive of a situation where men would take the place of women in many phases of our business and professional lives.

It is not my theory that women should abandon their role in the bearing and rearing of children; I believe that every young woman who has the potential should so plan her life that she can take her place in the business and professional world, if she desires such activities. Thus, she would be able to fill the long gap between the time her children are out of the way and old age.

As a further tribute to women and in support of my former statement of their superior moral character, I make the statement that every man's success depends upon some woman or women, either a mother or a wife or both, or perhaps a friend of strong character. I know by personal experience if I have amounted to anything, it is due to the influence of my mother, my wife and other women with whom I have come in contact. The older I get the more I appreciate women.

I believe in the old saying that "the hand that rocks the cradle rules the world." I often think of the philosophy in the old Negro song I heard many years ago that went like this: "Adam never had no mammy to teach him right from wrong. I know down in my heart he'd have left that apple be, but, you see, he never had no mammy to teach him right from wrong."

CHAPTER THIRTY-SEVEN
RELIGION AND PHILOSOPHY

I did not intend this work to have any religious overtones. My attitude toward religion and philosophy, whether it be Judeo-Christian, Buddhism, Mohammedanism, or the philosophy of Socrates and Confucius, is they are good if they make man better. I think, since man began to reason, they all had their place in the evolution of religion and the civilization of mankind.

Because of the nature of man, each of these beliefs was necessary to his development in its own era and locale. If it were a religion, it tied man to a belief in a Creator. If it were a philosophy, it developed a natural belief in right or wrong.

A famous writer, although an agnostic, said, "Because of the nature of man, I would hate to live in a world without religion." There are many things that motivate human activity. Some are motivated by fear, some by hope. At this point I refer to what I consider the four great sanctions. By sanction, I mean that which motivates or impels human conduct. Let us classify the four.

1. *Punitive sanction:* That which restrains evil conduct because of fear of punishment. A child may be restrained for fear of a spanking or denial of his wants. A mature person may be restrained from evil because of fear of eternal punishment as recounted in the Scriptures.

2. *Remunerative sanction:* A child may be good because he is promised a piece of candy. A mature person may be good because of the hope of reward inspired by the Biblical promises of eternal paradise.

148

3. *Sanction of Public Opinion:* A person may be restrained from evil conduct because of public opinion. "What will people say?", "What will people think?".

4. *Moral sanction:* The fourth, which I believe to be the most praise-worthy, I would describe as that which restrains evil conduct and impels good conduct due to one's philosophy of life. One acts upon his moral concept of right and wrong. Hence, one is not influenced in his acts either because of fear of punishment or hope of reward.

I dare say that ninety per cent of the readers of this will admit that their conduct is controlled by moral sanction as described above, and not by punitive sanction, remunerative sanction or that of public opinion.

My natural vanity may have caused me to think these concerns and interest in the various sanctions of conduct were original, had I not read from the learned historian, Will Durant, concerning the Arabian philosopher, Avicenna, who lived a thousand years ago. Durant said, "Avicenna achieved as well as any man the ever-sought reconciliation between the faith of the people and the reasoning of the philosophers. He did not wish, like Lucretius, to destroy religion for the sake of philosophy, nor, like al-Ghazali in the ensuing century, to destroy philosophy for the sake of religion. He treats all questions with reason only, quite independently of the Koran, and gives a naturalistic analysis of inspiration; but he affirms the people's need of prophets who expound to them the laws of morality in forms and parables popularly intelligible and effective; in this sense, as laying or preserving the foundations of social and moral development, the prophet is God's messenger. So Mohammed preached the resurrection of the body, and sometimes described heaven in material terms; the philosopher will doubt the immortality of the body, but he will recognize that if Mohammed had taught a purely spiritual heaven the people would not have listened to him, and would not have united into a disciplined and powerful nation. Those who can worship God in spiritual love, entertaining neither hope nor fear, are the highest of mankind; but they will reveal this attitude only to their maturest students, not to the multitude."*

Now I must pause to give religion credit, since I believe the moral principles of man today are the result of generations of religious teachings. I do not believe in arguments if the purpose of the argument is to destroy one's belief in a certain religion or philosophy of life.

I do not know where I read or heard the following story many years ago. You no doubt have heard or read of Bob Ingersol, a notorious agnostic who

---

*Durant, Will, *The Story of Civilization*, Vol. IV, Page 256, 1950.

lived three generations ago. He was a very brilliant man, but went about lecturing on agnosticism. Agnosticism is based on the theory that the origin and destiny of mankind is unknown and that theology does not give sufficient proof of either man's origin or his destiny. Ingersol held that these matters were unknown and would remain unknown.

Co-existent with Ingersol was a man by the name of Henry Ward Beecher, not a minister by profession but a layman of Brooklyn, New York, who devoted much of his life to religious teaching. According to the story, these two men were on a train together going from New York to Chicago to attend the Republican National Convention. When the conversation regarding politics and current events lagged, Beecher said to Ingersol, "Bob, I was in a big city the other day while it was snowing and sleeting. The streets were full of slush. In this difficult situation, I saw a man with one leg and one crutch trying to cross the street. Along came a big, burly fellow who knocked the crutch from under the cripple and left him sprawling in the snow. Bob, what do you think should be done to a man like that?" Bob Ingersol said, "He ought to be killed." Beecher said, "Bob, you are the man. Here is civilization struggling along, with its only crutch, Christianity, and you are constantly knocking that crutch from under it." The author of this story said that perhaps at that time Beecher had his doubts, but he was trying to support the faith that human beings had in a Superior Being, and not destroy it as was Ingersol.

I was reminded of the above story many years ago when traveling on a train from Dallas to Fort Worth. The train was fairly crowded. A Catholic nun entered and sat in the only vacant seat, next to me. Across the aisle was a very nice appearing middle-aged woman who later proved to be a very religious Baptist. In the seat with her was a nice looking and quiet young man. Directly behind the Catholic nun was an individual who was reading a book from the Smithsonian Institute, in which was a picture that was supposed to represent prehistoric man. He exhibited the picture to all within the hearing of his voice and said, "The very idea, claiming that God created anything that looked like that." As he spoke there came to my mind the thought that if that very fellow were turned loose in the wilderness without a shave, bath or haircut for six months, he would resemble the picture.

The point is he began his tirade about the fallacy of Judeo-Christian religion. He wanted everybody to know that, as far as he was concerned, it was a farce. I was glad to see the Baptist lady defend her belief quite well. The result was that the tirade became more heated. I finally asked the fellow what his background was. He said he was educated at a seminary as a Baptist preacher and pastored a large Baptist church for a long time, but finally realized it was all a farce. I asked, "Young man, what did they teach you in that seminary?" He answered, "Just the Bible. We were given no scientific education." I said, "I think that was your trouble. Had you been exposed to both theology and science at the same time, you would have been led to harmonize science with Genesis." The Catholic nun sitting next to me said, "When you study both science and religion in the proper context, you will find no conflict between the two." I replied, "I agree."

The train reached Fort Worth and the quiet young man and I got off. It was a very cold day, so I suggested that we go into a cafe for a cup of coffee. After we were seated he said, "I don't agree with that fellow. I believe in God." Then he continued, "I was an automobile salesman in New York City. I was doing well but got into the wrong company and became a hopeless alcoholic and was going to the dogs. I met a girl from a small town in Texas where there was no drinking. She married me and brought me to Texas. I now have a happy home and am doing well. I believe God had a hand in it." With this I agreed. I can only commend and not quarrel with Judeo-Christian faith. Has it not done more for the western world, the world that we know, than any other factor? How can I quarrel with Mohammed, Buddha, and Confucius? Did not the results of their lives and teachings uplift mankind? Neither can I quarrel with the infidel, atheist and agnostic, if they are intellectually honest. My only quarrel is with the iconoclastic methods of such men as Bob Ingersol and perhaps Tom Payne. Yet one must wonder with Isaiah, who said, "Who could have been God's teacher?" When we look at all the wonders of creation, too numerous to mention here, we wonder with Isaiah. It is understandable that when pre-historic man's mind began to develop to the point of understanding or wondering about the phenomena of the universe, he began to worship some idea or symbol of God.

I do have a quarrel with modern ecologists and the ways in which they operate. Creation came about somehow and men were given the minds to develop what the Creator had put here. Man has done great things for the welfare of mankind with the materials put here for his use.

I doubt if my father ever heard the word "ecology" in his whole lifetime. I have come to understand the word to mean the science of the study of the effect of the environment on all life from the smallest microbe to human beings. However, I say my father was an ecologist. I recall that when we settled on old Section 136 it contained rough land, many marshes, sloughs and swamps. His ecology taught him that while many of the natural environments were conducive to the development of crayfish, skunks, opossums and marsh snakes, it was necessary to drain and till the land in order to make the environment fit for the development of the spiritual and physical welfare of his family. I'm afraid that, unfortunately, many of the present day ecologists would not understand my father's ecological priorities.

Although my education was very meager as measured by standards of public schools, I was raised by the best of Christian parents. They taught reverence for the Bible and that disbelief would result in eternal condemnation. When I began to read and reason, I became concerned about an apparent conflict between orthodox religion and scientific facts.

Having been raised in a Baptist home where I was a regular attendant of church and Sunday School, naturally in my late teens, I joined the Baptist Young People's Union. Each Sunday night members were given a Biblical subject to discuss. One Sunday evening I was assigned the first chapter of Genesis. I did not want to refuse the assignment. However, you can imagine my dismay over the awesome responsibility. I had never before talked on my feet except in a third grade spelling class where I soon reached the foot of the line. Nevertheless, I tackled the job and gave it a lot of study in my untrained way.

I do not know whether it was because the news got around that ignorant LeRoy was going to make a speech, but a goodly crowd resulted that night. The school house used by the church on this particular night also contained a good percentage of deacons and a preacher or two. Most of them were literalists. And were they literalists!

I began what I thought was going to be a very learned and profound discourse as follows: "Now folks, there may be some who think there is a conflict between Genesis on the one hand and scientific facts and Darwin's theory of evolution on the other. However, you can see that there is no conflict if you read both in the proper context."

Well, the looks I got from my audience made me feel as if I was sinking through the floor and, although this was on a Sunday night over sixty years ago, I still have never finished that learned speech.

CHAPTER THIRTY-EIGHT

OPTIMISTIC VIEWPOINT

I do not share the pessimism that some entertain with reference to the so-called moral decay of the present generation. I have closely observed the conduct of four generations and I must say that I can see improvement and I think that my grandchildren and other young people are doing very well in this day and time, considering the conditions of our society. I believe that they will emerge and cope with changed conditions as they grow to understand themselves better.

I do not go along with the theory that the world is getting worse. The media keeps us constantly appraised moment by moment, hour by hour of the bad things that go on. The good things do not seem to be newsworthy. I will give an example.

In the small, sparsely settled community in which I was raised, merely a spot on the map, many things occurred which now would be flashed by television over the entire nation in a few hours. One incident which occurred about two miles from my home involved a husband and father of five children who had become so abusive to his family that the wife had to literally run him off. They lived as tenants on a large farm where there were two tenant houses. The other tenant's house was about a quarter of a mile away from the one in which they lived. It was unoccupied. The father came in the middle of the night and placed two sticks of dynamite under the house where he thought his wife and children were and blew the house to splinters. Then, learning that they had moved to the other house in his absence, he went there. Since he had no more dynamite, he knocked the door down and started to enter. The woman, who had no other protection, had taken an axe into the house and, when he broke in, she killed him with the axe.

About two miles away in another direction from my home, such strife had arisen between husband and wife that the husband left home leaving several daughters and two teenage boys. The wife divorced him and soon married again, very much to the displeasure of the divorced husband and the teenage boys. As a result of a plot between the father and one of the boys, the boy went to the grocery store and bought a bottle of strychnine, telling the merchant he wanted to poison wolves. On a Sunday morning, knowing that all of the people went to early mass and upon returning would always drink coffee, he rode back to the home, put the contents of the bottle of strychnine in the sugar bowl and rode away, intending to poison the entire family. It so happened that there was so little strychnine present that only one old woman, who had been brought home from church, died from the effect of the poison.

These incidents occurred three quarters of a century ago. If they had occurred today, the news would have been flashed over the news media for the whole country to hear. As I said before, the country was very thinly populated. Although perhaps the trend in reporting only bad news may be changing, I believe that now, with the dense population, if people were getting worse, many such incidents would be reported daily.

CHAPTER THIRTY-NINE

CONCLUSION AND ADVISE TO THE YOUNG LAWYER

If this work has been interesting to those who care to know how we lived three-quarters of a century ago and how dependent we were on Providence and the elements for our existence or, if reading about the duties of a country lawyer has been interesting, then I am glad I wrote it.

If the reader does not agree with the philosophy of this book, I have no quarrel with him. Religion and philosophy are personal matters and are entitled to constructive stimulation without argument or criticism.

To the young man contemplating practice of law, I will say that, although it is a profession involving much hard work, it has many compensations, all of which are not financial. I made the remark many times, often to the great disapproval of my younger friends, that money is not the sole purpose of the practice of law and that money is just the by-product of the lawyer's faithful service to mankind. It is my opinion that a lawyer, especially a country lawyer who has been granted the privilege of practicing law, owes a duty to other members of society. It is compensating to know that in every case you try, in every brief you prepare, and in every case consummated before the appellate courts, something has been added to the constant building of our system of justice. It may be hard not to take a little advantage now and then and not profit by the court and the adversary having overlooked some point in the adversary's favor. But, in the long run, complete honesty with regard to the facts of law applicable to the cases will pay off. Ultimate success will depend upon courts, clients and adversaries learning that you will always take an honest attitude regarding cases which you handle. I do not boast that

I have attained this position, but after 45 years in dealing with courts, clients and lawyers, I've been more and more convinced that this attitude is right.

Perhaps because I've always been closely identified with soil I've always been interested in the laws of real estate. To me, it seems that real estate contributes more to the wealth and welfare of mankind than any other element, except the elements of human energy and ingenuity. Lincoln was told when he began the practice of law a century and a half ago, that there was no more room in the profession. His answer was, "There's always room on top." I was told when I began the study of law that real estate was no longer important, because all real estate titles had been straightened out. I have found that advice to be very incorrect. Half a century ago it took a section of land to make title litigation worthwhile. Now, one acre in some instances is worth far more than a section was in those days. With the development of the country, many phases of the law of real estate have become important. The laws involving mineral rights, surface rights, water rights, rights of eminent domain, the partition of real estate among tenants and litigation over the title to real estate, the descent and distribution of real estate among the heirs of the deceased all have become important. The old principles of law must still be applied to these involved transactions. My son and I are now involved in many cases of this nature.

Probate law is another equally interesting and rewarding phase of the practice that has become not only involved and interesting but remunerative. The probate of estates has become more complicated over the years because of the federal and state inheritance tax, both of which now apply to the estates of most farmers and ranchers. It takes knowledge and skill to see that the tax collector does not get more than his fair share under the law.

It's always sad to contemplate the death of an old client but always gratifying if you can with fairness, honesty and expediency, upon his death, make a proper distribution of his estate among his loved ones to their satisfaction and in the way he wished it. Many of these wills were written years ago when the clients were young and poor. Now, because of their native industry and increase in the value of their property, some are wealthy. Unlike some lawyers, I have never been guilty of including instructions in the will which required the executor return to the lawyer who wrote the will to also have it probated upon death. But, they do come back. As a country lawyer practicing in one neighborhood over a long period of time, one forms relationships with more than one generation and ties that go beyond the ordinary relationship of attorney and client. I have experienced this and am grateful for it.

My advice to a young person contemplating the study of law would depend upon that person's goal in life and whether he was afraid of hard work and whether he realized that compensations are not all pecuniary. Personally, I have no regrets, so I say "Go ahead," if you can answer Kipling by saying, "Yes, I can walk with crowds and keep my virtue, or walk with kings and not lose the common touch. Neither foes nor loving friends can hurt me, and all men count with me but none too much . . .". If you can answer, "Yes, I can fill each unforgiving minute with sixty seconds worth of distance run," then I say "Go ahead, my son."

INDEX

A

A & P Company, 64
Alexander, Alex, 73, 74
Amarillo, Texas, 119
Amos & Andy, 101
Anahuac, Texas, 5, 33, 55, 102
Anahuac Lake, 33
Anahuac Oil Field, 55, 56
Arceneaux, Eunice Hamshire, 53
Arceneaux, Mr., 30, 31, 46
Arceneaux Ranch, 35, 93
Arkansas, 10
Aubey, Louis, 31, 32, 93
Austin, Stephen F., 14
Austin, Texas, 97, 98

B

Bailey, Joe, 95
Beall, A. H., 94
Beaumont Enterprise, 97
Beaumont-Hamshire Fig Co., 58, 63
Beaumont Irrigation Co., 55
Beaumont Rice Mill, 55
Beaumont, Texas, 9, 10, 15, 23, 26, 27, 33, 43,
    48, 54, 57, 58, 59, 63, 67, 71, 72, 90, 94, 96,
    97, 98, 101, 103, 114, 133
Beecher, Henry Ward, 150
Big Hill, 35
Bolivar Peninsula, 109, 114
Boston, Mass., 36, 57, 58
Boudreaux, Jules, 9
Broussard, Eloi, 53
Broussard, J. E., 55, 56
Broussard, Moise, 93
Burrell League, 15, 17

C

Caffall Carriage Co., 26
Canadian National Railroad, 63
Carpenter Fig Factory, 63
Carpenter, J. C., Co., 62
Caruthers, Edgar, 31
Central Park, 89
Chambers County, Texas 14, 15, 21, 33, 55,
    73, 78
Chicago, Ill., 101
China, 16
China Town, 90
Chirino League, 15, 17
Civil War, 7, 10, 17, 109

Columbia University, 95
Columbus, Texas, 14
Corsicana, Texas, 57
Cow Bayou, 8, 9
Craigen, Joe, 47
Crenshaw, Fred, 85
Crowley, Frank, 29
Curtis, B. R., 28

D

Daniels, C. B., 10
Denny, Will, 29
Denton, Texas, 13
Dowling, Dick, 7
Dunman, 109
Duran League, 15, 16
Dutch Joe, 35

E

Earl Carol's Vanities, 89
England, 102

F

Fannett, Texas, 10
Farmers' Cooperative Marketing Assoc., 103
Fence Lake, 35
Fischer, Otto, 13
Fisherman's Wharf, 36
Fort Worth, Texas, 10
Frank Keith Place, 14
"Frenchie," 67, 69
Friendswood, Texas, 62

G

Galveston, Texas, 11, 15, 16, 33, 94, 96, 109,
    113, 114
Galveston Daily News, 94
Garland Family, 28
Garner, Alice, 10
Garner, Annie, 10
Garner, Bradley, 8, 111
Garner, Jacob, 8-10
Garner, Jack, 9, 24
Garner, Molly, 9
Garner, Rachel, 8
Garner Ranch, 111
Garner, Sally, 9, 10
Garner, Sarah, 8, 9
Gilchrist, Texas, 114
Gill, George, 28, 47
Grant's Tomb, 90
Grimes & Hurst Drugstore, 48

Groves, Charlie, 28
Gulf and Interstate Railroad, 15, 16
Gulf Oil Company, 11

H

Hamshire Baptist Church, 82
Hamshire Fig Preserving Plant, 57
Hamshire, Lovan, 34, 53, 54
Hamshire, Texas, 10, 13-16, 18, 20, 25, 27, 30,
   31, 33, 34, 40, 43, 45, 53, 57, 58, 60, 63, 92,
   93, 96, 103, 113
Hankamer, Texas, 34, 93
Harris County, Texas, 111
Hebert, Ben, 46
Hebert, Joe, 53
Heisig, C. T., 58
High Island, Texas, 20, 109
Hoggatt League, 15-16
Houston, Texas, 55
Humble Company, 56

I

Ingersol, Bob, 150

J

Jackson, John, 73, 76, 77
Jackson's Ranch, 72, 73, 75, 77
Jean Lafitte Hotel, 109
Jefferson County, Texas, 7, 14-17, 54, 67, 97
Jenkins, Mr., 73, 76
Jennings, Louisiana, 70
Johnson, Ben, 8
Johnson, Brad, 9-10, 92
Johnson, Moise, 31-32
Johnson Place, 14
Jones, Buffalo, 15

K

Kansas, 8, 54
Kenneson family, 29
Koch, Theodore F., 60
Koch Land Co., 63, 96
Kountze Brothers, 24-25

L

LaSalle Correspondence School of Law, 95
Lawhon League, 15, 17
Lebanon, Tennessee, 95
Liberace, 49
Liggett, Francis J., 64
Little Pine Island, 54
Longfellow, Henry Wadsworth, 85
Lopez League, 15
Louisiana, 17, 66-68

Love, Fannie, 10
Lucas, 57

M

Mabry, Homer, 114
Mahaw Bayou, 28
Matagorda County, 112
McCall, Annie, 11
McCall, Alice, 5, 13, 79, 83
McCall, Cole, 113
McCall, David Eleric, 7, 11, 80, 81
McCall, Drew, 11
McCall, Eleric Webb, 13, 79, 83
McCall, Eva, 11
McCall, Jim, 7, 10
McCall, John, 7, 8,10, 11, 13, 14, 81
McCall, Julia Medlin, 13
McCall, Leroy, Jr., 6
McCall, Lovie, 13, 33, 42, 83
McCall, Maggie, 11
McCall, Martha Garner, 7, 8, 11, 80
McCall, Mary Sandell, 5
McCall, Mary Sue, 98
McCall's Nut House, 65
McCarthy, Glen, 56
McFarland League, 15
McGaffey, Charlie, 11
McGaffey, John, 8, 11, 40
McGaffey, Neil, 40
McReynolds, Arthur, 11
McReynolds, Major, 44
Memphis, Tennessee, 10
Mexico, 14, 15, 95
Mexico, Gulf of, 7, 20
Mississippi, 10, 11, 49
Mississippi River, 8, 10
Missouri, 27
Montreal, Canada, 36, 62
Mormon Temple, 49

N

Nacogdoches, Texas, 15
Neches River, 7, 55
New Orleans, Louisiana, 8, 14, 36, 54, 135
Newtown, Texas, 24
New York, 24, 64, 88, 89, 90, 135, 150
Nichols, Austin, 64
Nolte, Mr., 70
Nome, Texas, 15

O

Ogden, L. G., 33

159

Old Dan, 48
Old Pat, 104
Orange County, Texas, 8, 111
Orangefield, Texas, 8

P

Pavel, Mr., 9
Pearlstein Building, 98
Pennsylvania, 57
Philadelphia, Pennsylvania, 36
Pierce, Shanghai, 15, 109, 114
Pilat, Jack, 141
Pine Island Bayou, 55
Pineland, Texas, 132
Pipkin, Ben, 93
Pipkin, Bruce, 93
Port Arthur, Texas, 23, 25, 26, 59, 92, 97, 124
Pratt, Mrs., 92
Pujo, Louisiana, 132, 133

R

Railroad Avenue (Beaumont), 26
Rio Grande Valley, 60
Roberts, Mr., 74, 75, 76, 77, 78
Roedenbeck Farms, Inc., 56
"Roedenbeck Farms, Inc. vs. J. E.
    Broussard", 55
Roedenbeck, Herbert, 55

S

Sabine Lake, 7, 9
Sabine Pass, Texas, 7, 8, 9, 10, 11, 13, 14, 18,
    20, 23, 24, 25, 26, 33, 34, 35, 40, 41, 44, 57,
    82, 92, 93, 113, 114, 115
Sabine River, 7
Salt Bayou, 35
Santa Fe Railroad, 11, 132
Scoffield, Lovina, 93
Seaman Bros., 64
Skewbald, 46, 47
Smith League, 15, 17
Spencer, Junker, 93
Spindletop, 57, 59
Sterett Family, 34
Sterling, Governor Ross, 124
Stewart, Hiram, 11
Stillwell, 25
Stowell, Texas, 33, 34, 60
Stringtown, 93
Stringtown Community, 28
Sun Company, 9
Swartz, Sheriff, 70

T

Tarkington, Philip, 111

Tarkington's Prairie, 111
Taylor's Bayou, 23, 28
Taylor, C. Q., 28
Tennessee, 10
Texas, Republic of, 106
Texas Revolution, 14, 17, 106
Texas, State of, 14-16, 100
Times Square, 90
Trinity River, 21
Turtle Bay, 33
Tyree, Jim, 11

U

United States Census Bureau, 7
United States Government, 14

V

Vacocu League, 15
Valmore League, 15
Vaughn, Shirley, 5
Virginian, The, 137
Voiles, Jack, 97

W

Waldorf-Astoria, 35
Wall Street, 88
Washington, George, 20, 22
Washington-on-the-Brazos, Texas, 14
Webb, Bert, 10
Webb, Brenda, 31
Webb, J. M., 10
Webb, John, 20
Webb, Lizzie, 10
Webb, Lovie, 10, 11, 14
Webb, R. W., 10
Webb, Sue Green, 10, 80
Webb, Tommy, 45
Webb, W. J., 10, 14, 15, 45
West, Priscilla, 111, 112
White, R. M., 34
White's Ranch, 72, 74, 75
Wilber, Charles, 28, 93
Wilber, Stella, 93
Wilson, M. E., 60
Windsor Hotel, 36
Winnie, Fox, 15, 16
Winnie, Texas, 15, 16, 18, 21, 33, 60, 63, 76
Winnie Townsite Company, 16
Wister, Owen, 137
Work, Mr. 73-76, 78

Y

Yount, Frank, 58

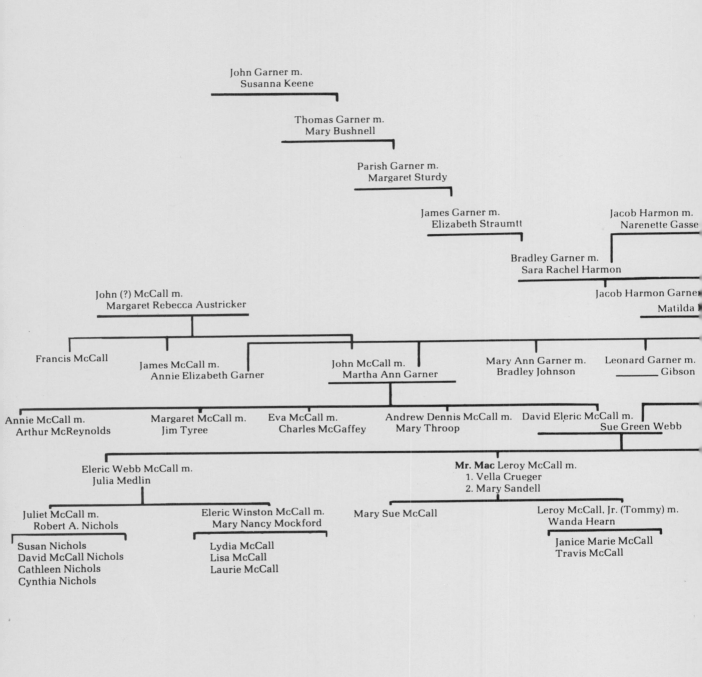

John Garner m.
Susanna Keene

Thomas Garner m.
Mary Bushnell

Parish Garner m.
Margaret Sturdy

James Garner m.
Elizabeth Straumtt

Jacob Harmon m.
Narenette Gasse

Bradley Garner m.
Sara Rachel Harmon

John (?) McCall m.
Margaret Rebecca Austricker

Jacob Harmon Garner
Matilda

Francis McCall

James McCall m.
Annie Elizabeth Garner

John McCall m.
Martha Ann Garner

Mary Ann Garner m.
Bradley Johnson

Leonard Garner m.
_____ Gibson

Annie McCall m.
Arthur McReynolds

Margaret McCall m.
Jim Tyree

Eva McCall m.
Charles McGaffey

Andrew Dennis McCall m.
Mary Throop

David Eleric McCall m.
Sue Green Webb

Eleric Webb McCall m.
Julia Medlin

Mr. Mac Leroy McCall m.
1. Vella Crueger
2. Mary Sandell

Juliet McCall m.
Robert A. Nichols

Eleric Winston McCall m.
Mary Nancy Mockford

Mary Sue McCall

Leroy McCall, Jr. (Tommy) m.
Wanda Hearn

Susan Nichols
David McCall Nichols
Cathleen Nichols
Cynthia Nichols

Lydia McCall
Lisa McCall
Laurie McCall

Janice Marie McCall
Travis McCall